THE SECRET

of

SUCCESS

by

R. C. ALLEN

BEST BOOKS INC.

P.O. Box 2309 — Henderson, Nevada 89015

Other writings by R. C. Allen

1953
Master Plan For Success

1955
How To Build a Fortune and Save on Taxes

1956
A Factual Record of 89 Insurance Stocks

1962
The Truth about Life Insurance

1976
Professional Trading Systems

How To Look and Feel 10 to 20 Years Younger — 1985

You Never Die — 1986

Immortal Words of Jesus Christ — 1984

R. C. ALLEN

P.O. Box 2309 • Henderson, Nevada 89015

Published simultaneously in Canada by
G. R. WELCH CO, Ltd.
Toronto, Canada

PRINTED IN THE UNITED STATES OF AMERICA
ISBN 0-910228-02-7

Dedicated To
The millions of people
Who believe in The Secret of Success

Wisdom is the principle thing
Therefore get wisdom
And with all thy getting
Get understanding.
Proverbs 4:7

Contents

1

Let There Be Light

MILLIONS of people are asking, "What is the Secret of Success and how can I obtain it?"

They want to *know* rather than guess. And many will gladly pay the price if it will produce a greater abundance of health, wealth and harmony in their lives.

Fortunately, there is nothing mysterious nor difficult about the way you can secure success. It is easier to obtain than many people realize. And the right answer is worth more than a hundred guesses.

Success, as you know, is the opposite of failure. It is the result of achieving respect, attention, greater freedom, good health, financial security and satisfaction in whatever you are doing. And, in a minor way, success is the result of doing something just a little better than someone else who believes the average is good enough.

Success comes easily and often to those who make an enthusiastic effort to serve and please others.

The man who starts a business of his own, satisfies his customers and adds more benefits to whatever he is selling, is a success.

The mother who teaches her children right from wrong and helps them grow up with a sincere desire to improve the world and serve the people around them, is a success.

The salesman who offers a worthwhile product or sells a service from which other benefit, is a success.

The secretary in an office, who does her work so well her boss thinks she is indispensable, is a success.

The farmer, who produces a high-quality crop, cultivates his land and raises fine cattle, is a success.

The guide, who is paid to direct a group of business and professional men to the best spot to hunt or fish, is a success.

The singer or musician, who helps to make the lives of others more pleasant, is a success.

And every wife is a success if she never loses faith in her husband and helps him reach out for better things.

Success, therefore, is the reward you receive for the time and effort you willingly give towards helping and serving other people. And the more people you serve and the better you perform that service, the greater your reward will be.

But *the greatest success* and *the most praise* is given to those men and women who make plans to serve and then continue to serve in spite of adversity, sickness, physical deformity, lack of cooperation and a shortage of money.

There are thousands of such individuals. No matter how difficult their problem may be and regardless of circumstances, they succeed because they have discovered *the Secret of Success*—which is available to all—not just a limited few.

As a result of learning and applying this *Secret of Success* millions of people can now succeed where only thousands have succeeded before.

Think a minute and consider these questions.

Why is it that some people are successful, while others are not? Why are a few people leaders, while others are followers? Why are some people happy and at peace with the world, while others so often worry, complain and grumble?

Why should such conditions exist? What makes one man or woman succeed, while others just wonder why?

The difference does not lie in education. Some of the greatest leaders and some of the most successful people the world has ever known have had little education as we know it today.

Education is a help, but it is not the answer.

Many well-educated people are not a success in the true sense of the word. Some have committed suicide in times of stress. Others complain of minor irritations that people with less education endure all day long.

The difference does not lie in physical strength nor in good health. Many deformed and handicapped people have accomplished great things.

An exploding bomb blew off both the hands of paratrooper Harold Russell during World War II. He had been looking forward to returning to his old job as a butcher. Without hands, however, he felt he had no hope and no future.

Army doctors fitted him with ingenious prosthetic appliances, metal fingers that enabled him to operate a typewriter, light a cigarette, thread a needle and do almost anything that others could do with fingers.

He was invited to make a training film to help other amputees. Then this former butcher boy received a contract to act in the motion picture, "The Best Years of Our Lives" for which he received an Academy Award. He later became a leader in the Disabled Veterans Organization and lectured all over the United States.

When Harold Russell was asked if he regretted his condition, he replied, "No, my deprivation had been my greatest blessing. What counts is not what you have lost but what you have left."

Annette Kellerman and Franklin D. Roosevelt were both stricken with polio. It could have slowed their progress or darkened their spirits. But Annette Kellerman overcame her handicap to become the greatest swimmer and the most beautiful woman of her time. And Franklin D. Roosevelt revived our spirits during the worst depression in history with the words, "We have nothing to fear, but fear itself."

And hard work is not the answer. Many men and women spend long hours in physical labor, but they find it even harder to make a living. Others find time to play golf and fish, yet they seem to make a living without much effort.

Success and happiness, you will find, are neither helped nor handicapped by the environment in which you live. Abraham Lincoln, Booker T. Washington and Andrew Carnegie rose to great heights in spite of their lowly birth and tremendous handicaps.

The Secret of Success is not something new. It is not, in any way, reserved for a few. It has been with us since time began. And, the more you understand and accept it, the more easily it will help you. New opportunities will open up and they will lead you to more successful achievements.

If you will carefully read each page in this book, then have persistent *faith,* follow through and *believe—*

> you will learn how to use more of the tremendous power within you to achieve greater self-confidence, move ahead in your job, find new health, increase your earnings, improve your relations with others—and achieve any form of success you strongly desire—*more easily.*

Many books attempt to show the way to success but they fail to show how success can be made both permanent and complete.

Some of the books you read will explain how to make more money. But they neglect to point out why it is also important to have *peace of mind.* Other books illustrate how you can secure *peace of mind* but they make no effort to show you how to increase your income.

For those reasons, a need arose and this book was written to give you the ever-lasting *Secret of Success* that will never fail you—once you learn it and apply it. It is the answer everyone wants—regardless of age, environment or circumstances.

The Truth is—anyone who knows how can succeed.

Why, then are there so many people who are frustrated? Why do so many people fail? Why do so many others worry and complain about their "problems?"

The reason is—they have not learned how to work in harmony with *the Secret of Success* which is—

"Seek ye *first* the Kingdom of God
and His righteousness; and all good
things shall be added unto you."*

This *Secret of Success* never fails. It is the one thing you can always depend upon to bring harmony, peace of mind, order and justice into your life—more easily.

When you understand it, believe it and follow it, all of your problems, worries and frustrations fade away. Your life improves and you begin to enjoy a greater amount of security, personal satisfaction, good health and friends.

Helen Keller was born in the little town of Tuscumbia, Alabama. When only 19 months old, she was stricken with a fever and became blind and deaf. At the age of three, she also became mute. But she rose above her triple handicap to become one of the best known individuals in the world and an inspiration to everyone who met her.

With great difficulty and hours of practice each day, she learned to speak. She read books in Braille for such long periods of time, her fingers bled and had to be covered with silk for protection.

Deeply spiritual, she prayed often and felt her mission in

---

* Matthew 6:33

life was to help others who were blind and deaf and needed the encouragement to work and carry out their lives with full responsibility rather than live off charity.

At the age of 20, she entered Radcliffe College in Massachusetts. In spite of being unable to see, hear or speak, her determination to succeed and her perseverance helped her to acquire the knowledge necessary to graduate with honors.

The Bible, of course, gives *the Secret of Success.* Many people who read It, however, fail to understand and grasp the spiritual power and wisdom it contains. Some even try to deny it.

But—*the Truth is*—miracles *can* happen and *do* happen many times for all those who have enough *faith* and the wisdom to *believe.*

Over and over again, *the Secret of Success* has helped to make the lives of such people easier. In spite of financial problems, adverse criticism and lack of cooperation, they discovered that, whenever they give close attention to *the Secret of Success,* they have found the money they need, the right marriage partner and the *peace of mind* that is so important to all those who *desire* a rich and satisfying life.

That is why, when anyone says to them, "Show me and I will believe," they can give this answer with sincerity and conviction.

I *believe* because I *know.*

I have been shown.

To get the most out of this book, read each chapter with an open mind.

An open mind looks for and accepts new ideas. A closed mind resents them.

Albert E. Wiggam, the famous psychologist, said, "The line between 'open-mindedness' and 'tight-mindedness' is sharp and clean cut—and the only people who have ever contributed anything to human progress have been the 'open-minded' who have been able to see there is a better way."

Most people long to know why any given fact is true. Some, however, boast of an "open mind" yet wind up with a "closed mind."

When a discussion is started, they listen eagerly and with interest so long as their own viewpoint is discussed. As soon as someone makes a statement contrary to what they believe or a remark is made, "there is a better way," their minds are closed immediately. They feel there is no longer any need to discuss it.

Such an attitude, obviously, results in a closed mind.

Bishop Fulton J. Sheen wrote, "Those who boast of open-mindedness are invariably those who love to search for truth, but not to find it. They love the chase for truth, but not the capture. Many people keep their minds open to truth—but fail to close them in time to grasp it."

True open-mindedness means you must be willing to listen to everyone who proposes a new idea or expresses a thought and allow them the opportunity to explain it.

Then, after they have finished, discuss it fairly, find out the good points and add those good points to your growing storehouse of information.

This book should be read with such an open mind. It can change and improve your life because, within these pages, you will find many statements of *Truth* that can help you to understand life more easily. And the dividends you receive from *the Secret of Success* will be greater peace of mind, new ideas and a larger amount of income for the services you render.

Some people, however, believe that success is proven when you have a fine home, fancy clothes and a lot of money.

While money is important, it is not a true measure of success. And it can never buy true love, happiness nor peace of mind.

Money is nothing more than the payment you receive for the help and service you give to others. And the more help and service you give, the greater the amount of money you will receive in return.

It should never be considered a permanent asset because it can fade away for many reasons. There are individuals in all walks of life who experience financial difficulties no matter how large or small their incomes may be. Bankruptcies occur among large companies and small companies in every area of the world. Inflation can eat up much of your savings. And the stock market can go down.

At such times, *the Secret of Success* is the only thing you can turn to and rely upon for the courage, the faith and the inspiration you need to face the future.

"Money," Benjamin Franklin said, "Never made a man happy, nor will it. There is nothing in the nature of money to produce happiness. The more a man has, the more he wants. Instead of filling a vacuum, it makes one."

The person you consider successful from a material standpoint may be unhappy from a spiritual standpoint. He may be grouchy, irritable and selfish. He may have few dependable friends. And he may suffer from high blood pressure, headaches and ulcers.

His unhappiness shows up in his face and his attitude. The reason is—he lacks the *peace of mind* which comes from understanding and *believing* in *the Secret of Success*.

His attention is centered on elusive, material things such as money and the pursuit of pleasures that can be lost overnight instead of the more dependable spiritual values which are never lost but remain forever.

In the final analysis, you will find that money is not your primary desire in life. Everyone in this world—the million-

aire with his fine home and the lowly savage in the jungle—
has only one desire. It is fundamental and never changes.
Good times or bad times, peace or war, your primary desire
is—*to have peace of mind and live a happy life in comfort.*

Some people call this "paradise." And very few ever find
it. But those who understand and demonstrate their belief
in *the Secret of Success* will own a greater portion of this
paradise than those who "don't care" or "don't believe."

The Truth is—logic and common sense will always prove
the wisdom of the statement—

> "Wealthy is the man
> who has peace of mind."

It is the most valuable and dependable possession you can
ever own.

Without *peace of mind,* all other treasures are of small
value. It is the ultimate good, "the pearl of great price," yet
it cannot be purchased. It can only be secured by those who
desire it above all else in the world.

The Secret of Success helps you secure and enjoy this
ever-dependable *peace of mind.* It enables you to live a
happy life—regardless of the amount of money you have.
And it encourages you to work more closely with God.

It gives you confidence and points out why the more
you give of yourself to the world in the way of services and
goods, the more peace and security you will get out of it.

There are a limited number of people who believe so
devoutly in this *Secret of Success* that their constant attention to its precept has exalted them into saints. No matter
what obstacles are placed in their way, they succeed because
they work closely with God and reap the many blessings that
result.

As you read through this book, you will find that miracles

can happen when you know how to use this *Secret of Success*. But do not expect miraculous results overnight. Mortal man cannot perfect anything in a single day. And a bird cannot fly until its wings have developed enough to support its body.

Remember it takes time for eggs to hatch. It takes time to learn to play the piano. It takes time to make a journey of a thousand miles. And it takes time to go from ordinary success to greater success.

A great deal depends on how eager you are to "Seek *first* the Kingdom of God" and how willing you are to follow the suggestions and leads you are given.

You may be certain that life will improve for everyone as soon as men and women all over the world, who have influence, can teach and inspire others to believe that—

> *the Secret of Success is a close and constant relationship with the infinite wisdom and creative spirit of God and God is the Secret of Success.*

The closer and more constant this relationship with **God** —*the Secret of Success*—the easier it will be for answers to problems to come from the most intelligent and dependable source. Miracles and many wonderful things can then happen.

Harmony and freedom will increase. All of the ills, crimes and oppressions that exist will begin to fade away. And peace and justice will be expressed and experienced more often by everyone.

2

The Secret Revealed

Your body is a remarkable creation but, physically, you possess no ability that cannot be equalled or surpassed by the humblest of animals.

You are not as strong as a gorilla, as swift as a rabbit nor as graceful as a deer. You can not see as well as a bird nor can you hear as well as a dog.

And, in proportion to your size, you are not as strong as an ant nor can you jump as high as a grasshopper.

The chemist knows that your body consists mostly of water and a variety of chemicals that can be purchased for less than a dollar. Yet man has risen higher than any other creature.

Why? What is the secret?

The supremacy you possess over animals does not lie in your body. It comes from an Infinite Intelligence and Creative Spirit that enables you to use your brain more efficiently and helps you accomplish whatever you want—more easily.

Many thousands of years ago, certain wise men became conscious of this creative spirit and found that it helped them solve their problems and overcome all obstacles when everything else failed.

They could not define this dependable power but they reasoned and believed that it was of Divine origin.

They discovered they could always rely upon It whenever emergencies arose.

This awakening and a belief in a Power greater than

themselves became the starting point in man's supremacy over his fate and his destiny.

Ever since man first realized this power existed, he began to evolve faster and more easily. His spirit rose ever higher from savagery towards the beautiful and perfect soul for which man has always been intended.

Certain enlightened individuals found that, whatever they could visualize or imagine, could be transformed into reality with the help of this Infinite Wisdom and Power.

They found that, whatever they thought about they could do. They also found that, by directing their thoughts, they could affect the people and things around them.

Evil men found they could create evil things. Power-hungry men, like the Pharoahs of Egypt, Genghis Khan, Napoleon and Hitler, took over the leadership of their countries and attempted to create the impression that they and their group were more important than God.

But their power structures lacked the proper foundation.

They were overthrown and, in many cases, their downfall caused their countries to suffer along with them.

Good men, however, like Moses, Confucius, Buddha, Mohammed, Gandhi and, especially, Christ, created good things. And the spiritual legacy they gave to the world enables other men to build a better civilization based on the moral values they were given.

Your brain is a remarkable instrument but, by itself, it cannot think. It cannot create ideas nor cause your body to move.

If your brain had the ability to think and create ideas, then it could also think after it had been removed from your body.

It is logical, then, to believe that there is an Infinite Mind—a Creative Source of wisdom and intelligence that uses your brain as an instrument or channel. It activates your brain and gives you the ability to think and the potential to "accomplish all things."

When you ask yourself the following questions you find there is only one logical answer.

What makes the sun rise and set every day so precisely that you know exactly six months from now—even ten years from now, by looking at an almanac, when it will rise and set again?

What causes the blade of grass to grow and inspires the tiny acorn to expand into an oak tree one hundred feet tall?

What is so wise it knows every second of your life exactly how to run such a complex machine as your body?

What is it that can take a mixture of bread, meat and potatoes and, with remarkable efficiency, turn them into blood, skin, bone, hair and fingernails?

What is so alert it keeps your heart beating regularly every second of your life—whether you are asleep or awake?

What is so reliable it knows exactly how to heal a cut finger, knit a broken bone, or cure a cold?

Surely you cannot do any of those things yourself.

That is why it is so easy to believe there is an efficient, powerful, all-knowing and ever-present Creative Spirit and Infinite Intelligence that directs and controls every tiny atom in the entire Universe.

This ever-present source of wisdom and power is *the Secret of Success*—your Super-Conscious (Creative) Mind. It is "The Kingdom of Heaven," Christ said, "is within."

It is so dependable that, with Its help and guidance, you can more easily secure all of the *peace of mind,* money and happiness you will ever need or want.

It will help you succeed in spite of any handicap you may have or any circumstance in which you find yourself.

It gave men like Leonardo di Vinci, Christopher

Columbus, Benjamin Franklin, Thomas A. Edison and Werner Von Braun the ability to see and do things the average man of their time believed were impossible.

By the time you finish this book, you will know and understand why your Super-Conscious Mind is everything. In fact, there is no limit to what your Super-Conscious Mind can do to help you once you know how to use It.

Through the nerves and cells that comprise your brain, this Creative Source of Power causes your conscious mind to think and work on every idea you are given so that you can encourage others and help them perfect every material thing within the entire Universe.

This Creative Source of Power is known by many names —God, Divine Mind, Super-Conscious Mind, Infinite Mind, Creative Spirit, Supreme Intelligence, Universal Mind, etc.

Those names shall be used interchangebly throughout this book, but no matter how you say them, they are all one and the same.

You will soon learn how you can "tune in" this Infinite Power and use more of Its tremendous, unlimited resources to get all of the things you need and sincerely *desire* —love, money, a better job, business success, everlasting *peace of mind* and the right answer to any problem you may have—no matter how difficult that problem may be.

Yes—all of those things are possible. And the reason is—psychologists have found that the average person uses only 10% of his mind's capacity. 90% goes unused.

Imagine the miracles you can accomplish when you learn how to "tune in" your Super-Conscious (Creative) Mind and use another 10%—even better—another 50%.

You can see why there is no question you can do more to improve your life. And you can always become a greater success.

But first you must have *an intense and active desire* to do so because "faith without works is dead."

The more often you "Seek *first* the Kingdom of God" and turn to *the Secret of Success* for guidance, the more certain your success will be. And whatever good things you need in life will eventually work out in your favor.

Many people ask, "Which came first—the chicken or the egg?" But, rather than spend time on the question which came first, it would be wiser to ask, *"How* did the Infinite Intelligence create the chicken or the egg?"

Certain scientists have searched all over the world to find "the missing link" in an effort to prove their feeble contention that man may have descended from monkeys.

They overlook *the Truth* that the missing link they need to acknowledge is God.

If they will agree that the Infinite Intelligence could create a monkey, a horse or an elephant—then certainly they must agree that Its infinite wisdom could also create a man.

Some people however say, "I don't believe in God."

But it is easy to prove that God exists. If a man were to try to create a human being, what a pitiful result he would get. Without God as the creator and director, our bodies would be nothing but inefficient, misshapen monstrosities.

In addition to the blood and nerves and organs, the unfailing creative spirit necessary to build and heal our bodies would be impossible to create and perfect.

If you ask such non-believers to explain why a seed of corn does not produce a tomato, they will reply, "Well, corn is supposed to produce corn."

But, if a Divine Intelligence were not guiding the growth of the cells in that seed of corn, occasionally, it might produce a pineapple or a pear.

Corn seed, however, will always produce corn, acorns will produce oak trees and we human beings will produce human beings. All in a logical, predictable manner.

In his book, "A Reporter Looks at God," Howard Whitman wrote, "The young scientist may be cocksure in his laboratory and say 'How wonderful I am. Look what I've found in the atom.' The older scientist, however, will say, 'Isn't God wonderful—look what He's put in the atom.'"

The *Truth* is vitally important. That is why Christ said, *"Ye shall know the Truth and the Truth shall make you free."*

If knowing *the Truth* can produce the peace of mind and freedom from worry and want that is so important, then it is logical to assume there is a scientific law you can use that will automatically help you when you know how to use it.

That Law is known to every enlightened man and woman as "The Law of Universal Mind (God) in Action."

There is no limit to what the mind and spirit of God, this Universal Mind can accomplish.

Many individuals, however, often limit themselves by failing to turn to It and use Its infinite wisdom to help them solve their problems and enjoy a life filled with a greater portion of health, wealth and happiness.

When you increase your *desire* and make an effort *to serve more people,* then back it up with persistent *faith* and *belief* in *the Secret of Success,* your life will improve and it will be easier to reach your goal.

As you learn more about *the Secret of Success* and how It can guide your life, you will know how to use more of this Infinite Creative Power within your mind. You will know and understand why every obstacle and every problem you experience can be overcome.

A business depression will not upset you. Unhappiness will not occur. Periodic cycles of trouble will pass away and worries and frustrations will disappear.

Many people, unfortunately, doubt that is possible. They feel that what cannot be seen cannot be believed.

But, *the Truth is*—miracles have happened and will continue to happen so long as men continue to have *faith* and *believe* in an Infinite Power which is greater and more dependable than their own.

Christ inspired the hopeless cripple when He said, "Do you believe? Then take up your bed and walk."

He gave new life to Lazarus when He said, "Arise."

And he proved there is no limit to the amount of substance that is available when God is asked to supply it for He took the five loaves and two small fishes, blessed them and fed the multitude.

Jesus was a Man of Action. He *understood* the unlimited wisdom and Creative Spirit of Good. And He *believed* that God would never fail Him and would always provide whatever He needed.

If His understanding had been limited to what He saw, then instead of accomplishing "miracles," He would have sympathized with the cripple and said, "I'm sorry to see you cannot walk." He would have looked at Lazarus and said, "It's too bad he died." And, to the multitude who were hungry, He might have said, "They will have to do without."

But He *knew* that God would always supply the needs of those who love Him and respect Him.

He *understood*. He had *faith*. And He put into practice what He *believed*. That is why, as a Man of Action, He was successful.

Some people say, "Seeing is believing." But *the Truth is*—your eyes cannot see many of the things that actually exist. In fact, many of the things you cannot see have more power and importance than those things you can see.

You cannot see the force of gravity, nor the oxygen you breathe, but they exist for without gravity you would float around helplessly in space and without oxygen you would die.

You cannot see the electricity that lights up your home. Nor can you see the life-giving substance in the water you drink.

You cannot see the pictures that are sent through the air,

but your television set reproduces them clearly. You cannot see the sounds coming from a broadcasting station, but your radio makes it possible to hear those sounds.

You cannot see the ultra-violet rays that tan your skin. And you cannot see the vitamins and minerals that are present in the food you eat.

Your eyes, therefore, are not as dependable as you would like them to be.

You have *faith* that gravity will hold you in contact with the ground. You have *faith* that the oxygen you breathe will give you energy and life. You have *faith* that when you turn on the switch, the electricity will cause your television to work. And you have *faith* that the lifeless looking food you eat will nourish you.

As soon as you realize how many of your abilities are limited and why persistent *faith* and *belief* in a greater Wisdom and Power is so important you can easily accept the fact that God is always ready and willing to help you.

All you need to do is—"Ask and it shall be given you; seek, and ye shall find; knock and it shall be opened unto you."*

While that is true, many people do not understand this *Secret of Success*. When they have problems that trouble them, they turn to a psychoanalyst for help. Others change jobs, take a vacation or move to a new location in an effort to eliminate the problem.

There may be times when it is helpful to turn to an outside source but running away from a problem will not solve it. The problem will remain and it will continue to follow them, in one form or another, until their attention is turned to the Right Source for help.

People who understand *the Secret of Success* know

---

* Matthew 7:7

that "the Kingdom of Heaven is within". By relaxing and listening carefully to their Super-Conscious Mind, they feel confident they will receive the right answer and their difficulties can then be overcome more easily.

Below is a list of some of the men and women who found this *Secret of Success* and kept it constantly in mind.

You will notice that each of these men and women became famous in spite of their handicaps. Many had little education. The majority faced ridicule because of their beliefs. And they all started with a limited amount of money.

Yet, by knowing *the Secret of Success* and believing in a power greater than themselves, they accomplished everlasting fame.

(This is only a partial list—there are many thousands more)

Christ	Ralph Waldo Emerson
Moses	Thomas A. Edison
Solomon	Henry Ford
Socrates	Alexander Graham Bell
Saint Peter	Florence Nightingale
Saint Paul	Andrew Carnegie
Confucius	Joan of Arc
Buddha	Brigham Young
Mohammed	Booker T. Washington
Sir Francis Bacon	Mary Baker Eddy
Martin Luther	Luther Burbank
John Wesley	Myrtle Fillmore
Leonardo Di Vinci	Parmahansa Yogananda
Saint Augustine	Emmet Fox
Galileo	Charles Fillmore
Saint Francis of Assisi	Eddie Rickenbacker

Michaelangelo	Ernest Holmes
Mary Bethune	Billy Graham
Walter Russell	Frank Buckman
Herbert Hoover	Douglas McArthur
Albert Schweitzer	Norman Vincent Peale

Whatever the above men and women have done, it is possible for you to do also. And, if you have enough *faith* and *desire* and keep in constant touch with this *Secret of Success* then, as Christ pointed out, "Even greater things shall ye do."

As you learn more about *the Secret of Success* and *understand* how Its creative spirit and infinite wisdom can work in your life, you will find that success in your affairs comes more easily. The reason is, as Christ explained, "*All things are possible to him that believes.*"

Paul Harvey in one of his broadcasts said, "Let's face it—no man ever 'invented' anything. All the brains of M.I.T., the Bell Telephone Laboratories, General Electric and our institutes of aeronautical research have never invented anything. We just 'discovered' certain things. The elements of electricity and radio, television and jet propulsion have all been here since the beginning of time. But for each generation, the curtain has been parted a little farther to reveal more of those things that were there all along."

When the great athlete, Bob Richards, received an award as the amateur athlete of the year, he was asked by reporters for the secret of his success in athletics. He told them, "I owe my achievements to the power of the Lord. The psychological influence which He exerts over all those who search their souls and find there the strength to perform wonderful things."

As the years go by, more men and women *understand* and use this Law of Universal Mind and are accomplishing the "greater things" that Christ told us could be done.

Until 1932, all the books on physics said, "Every bit of matter can be broken down into atoms, but you cannot split an atom." The books based on the limited knowledge of mortal men, stated that as a fact.

But it was not a fact. The infinite spirit and creative wisdom of God is more complex and greater than they realized.

Today, we not only split atoms, we are using the energy hidden within those atoms to accomplish many new miracles of power. With the power of Infinite Intelligence helping us to accomplish all things, there is no limit to what we can achieve in the future—if we will express enough *faith*, have the *desire* and *believe*.

On July 15th, 1965, the United States spacecraft, Mariner IV, had traveled over 134 million miles and taken photographs of the planet Mars. The fact that a man-made object could travel such a great distance under perfect control and timing helps scientists prove that the spirit of God is everywhere and His power and influence extend far beyond this earth.

Trees grow and bear fruit because the Infinite Intelligence directs the action of every cell in each tree, every second of every day, from its root to its top.

If you plant an apple tree, you know it will bear apples—not peaches. If you plant tomatoes, you will get tomatoes—not beans. If you plant roses, you will get roses.

When you go to sleep at night, you know that your heart will continue to beat, your blood will continue to circulate and every cell in your body will carry on the work it is intended to do—all in perfect harmony without your direction.

You understand those facts are true and it is easy to believe them when you realize that the infinite wisdom and creative spirit of God controls and directs the action and production of every material thing that exists.

So long as a tree or a plant is allowed to grow naturally, it will fulfill its mission in life, but if a cover is placed over that tree so the sun and air cannot reach it, that tree becomes stunted, diseased and it may soon die.

When that cover is removed, the tree or plant will get its alloted share of sunshine, air and water. Then, even though it has been stunted, it will perk up again and grow.

And so it is in your own life. If you shut out the creative spirit and tremendous power of your Super-Conscious Mind so that it cannot flow easily and naturally throughout your mind and body, you will find it is much harder to accomplish the things you want to do.

It makes no difference what your religion may be. All religions teach the same basic truth—that there is an Infinite, All-Powerful Spirit that is known as God.

The way to "tune in" this Infinite Mind has never been taught to the majority of people. To date, it has never been taught in schools because it was believed that "no one's mind can understand *the Truth* until that mind is ready to receive it."

As a result of such a belief, this knowledge has been kept a "secret" and given only to those enlightened men and women down through the ages who were willing and eager to advance towards a higher plane in life.

Today, people are wiser. They are more alert and more willing to accept the viewpoints of others—if they believe those views have merit. They want to know *the Truth* and eagerly search for ways to find it.

Until this book was written, the facts you will read, could be found only in secret archives, discussed by groups of advanced thinkers or taught in special classes to those who were ready and willing to find the light.

The principles involved in these "secrets" have been taught by all of the world's greatest teachers. My only purpose is to *simplify* what they have taught—to help you understand their lessons more clearly and show you additional ways you can use those lessons to bring you more of the good things you desire.

It is easier to understand this *Secret of Success* when you realize that there is no such thing as *your* mind, *my* mind, *his* mind or *her* mind. Your mind, my mind and everybody's mind are simply outlets from the one Universal Mind that is the Author and Creator of all things.

You will find that your mind and the mind of every individual in this world are like the electrical outlets that branch off from a power line and enter a house. Each individual outlet can light up the house but the power to produce that light can come only so long as it is connected with the central powerhouse.

If you turn off the switch, no current will flow and you will receive no light. And, if you close your mind to the Central Powerhouse, which is the infinite wisdom and creative spirit of God, the power and light It has to offer to enrich your life will be "short-circuited" and It cannot flow easily into your conscious mind.

The Secret, you see, is simple.

As you understand how electrical power can be received and used, you can more easily understand how the Law of Universal Mind can be received and used to help you solve your problems and make your life worthwhile.

This Universal Mind is present within you every second of every day. It is an ever-active principle of *good* to be drawn upon and used to help you in every way—no matter how small that way may seem.

To enjoy a greater measure of success, all you need to do is to make certain you are in close and constant contact with this infinite wisdom and creative spirit.

The electric light switch in your house is like your brain.

It has no power by itself. It cannot create light nor create a picture on your television screen. The power comes from the central power plant.

No matter how much you desire light in your home or want a picture on your television screen, you will not get that light or picture until, *first,* you turn on the switch that connects your house with the central power plant from which the actual power flows.

The electrician knows how to repair an electric light switch because he has studied the principles of electricity and he knows that, when certain rules are followed, the electric current will always flow easily and smoothly.

So long as the proper connection is made between the outlets in your home and the central powerhouse, then both light and power are always available. If the wires are ever crossed, a short-circuit occurs. If a connection is broken, the central powerhouse will still exist but no power will flow into your home through that line.

The above illustration was given to help you understand more clearly the relationship between your conscious mind which is limited in its ability and your Super-Conscious Mind which is infinite and can help you to know and accomplish all things.

It is "The Truth," that Christ said, "shall make you free."

In Chapter Six, you will learn how to "tune in" this Infinite Mind and receive more of the power and wisdom it has to offer.

Since *"the Truth shall make you free,"* it is easy to realize that, whenever you want freedom from tension, worries and problems, you must be aware of the fact such freedom is possible.

When your mind is continuously in touch with the Universal Mind, your thoughts will be filled with the uplifting, energizing spirit you receive from that Mind. Your tension, worries and problems can then disappear.

An Infinite Mind with a greater wisdom and ability than your own will take over and It will show you how you can solve those problems. Then freedom, peace of mind and a successful life are the natural results.

In a large measure, you are responsible for the conditions under which you live. No situation is "hopeless" and, with God's help, every unfortunate condition can be improved.

If your life is pleasant and prosperous, then you have learned a great deal about the *Secret of Success*. If, on the other hand, the conditions under which you live are unpleasant and you experience hardship and lack, then you can easily improve those conditions as you learn more about this *"Truth that can set you free."*

If your mind should dwell upon fear, you will eventually experience conditions of fear. You will be enslaved by those fears and you will not be "free." If you let your mind dwell upon failure and lack, you will eventually experience conditions that will produce such failure and lack.

If you constantly think of success, *desire* success and actively pursue the goal you keep in your mind, you will eventually be successful.

If you constantly think of prosperity, see yourself having more money and have a *desire* for more money, more money will eventually come to you.

And, if you constantly think of love and happiness, then love and happiness will become a normal part of your life.

As soon as you concentrate your time and attention on positive, God-inspired thoughts, those thoughts which are negative and self-defeating will disappear. Then you will no longer experience worry, fear, sickness and lack.

In their place you will have peace of mind, greater freedom and a better way of life.

In other words, as soon as you "Seek *first* the Kingdom of God," your life begins to improve and "all good things shall be added unto you."

When you know and understand this *Secret of Success* and enthusiastically turn to the Infinite Mind for help, you will receive more of the many blessings It has to offer.

It will give you the ideas and the answers you need to create new things and solve your problems. And It will supply you with the physical power and mental ability to carry out those ideas to a successful conclusion.

But when you turn your mind away from this *Secret of Success,* you allow the contact to be broken and you are unable to receive the full amount of power and help It is so willing and able to give.

You are, in effect, saying, 'My will, not Thy will, be done."

If your connection with that Mind is corroded by wrong thoughts, hate, resentment, criticism or anger, you will have a poor reception from that source of wisdom and power. You will then experience many periods of unhappiness, sickness and financial problems.

Fortunately, you can correct such conditions.

The electrician knows that when a line is broken, it can be repaired. If a wire is corroded, it can be cleaned.

You can repair the line between your conscious mind and your Super-Conscious Mind or you can keep putting it off until many days and weeks have passed.

The longer you wait to make certain that the connection is complete and all the corroded parts (wrong thoughts) have been cleaned, the longer it will be before you can enjoy the creative spirit and tremendous power that will flow into your conscious mind from this all-knowing, wonder-working and infinite Super-Conscious Mind.

The fact that you have read this far and believe these

words *proves* that there is already within you a spiritual understanding which knows these words to be *true*.

As you become more conscious of the *Truth* and understand more clearly how your Super-Conscious Mind works, you will realize how close you are to this Universal Power.

Eventually, you will become so conscious of Its ability to help you accomplish all things that, instead of thinking of this Infinite Source of Power as being somewhere "far off" "above," or unavailable you will, instead feel It and know It to exist nowhere else but *deep within your own mind*.

Then you will know and UNDERSTAND the importance of *the Secret of Success* which Christ taught when He said, "The Father within, He doeth the works."*

---

* John 14:10

3

The Wonderful Power
You Possess

I T is significant that the first four words in the Bible are—
"In the beginning God."*

The Truth is—you have a marvelous creative spirit and wonder-working power within you which can improve your present circumstances and re-shape your future.

When you are in close and constant contact with this infinite source of all wisdom and power—which is God—your Super-Conscious Mind, there is no limit to what you can accomplish.

You are, in fact, capable of greater things than you now believe. And you can accomplish those things—more easily.

As Shakespeare so wisely put it, "The fault, dear Brutus, lies not in our stars, but in ourselves, that we are underlings."

The more often you think about the tremendous power and ability of your Super-Conscious Mind, the more easily you can express it. And the more strength and courage you will receive to help you stand firm against any of the problems and difficulties you may experience. Harold Russell and Helen Keller whom you met in Chapter One proved this.

---
* Genesis 1:1

No matter how successful you may be at this moment, some circumstance may occur that can cause you to lose everything you own in a single day.

A fire, flood, earthquake, tornado, war or bankruptcy can deprive you of a lifetime of savings and hard work. You may even lose all of your children or other members of your family in a serious accident. In spite of that loss, however, you can still rise above the unfortunate mental upset that can occur, if you will remember the wonder-working power of *the Secret of Success* and use It to regain your sense of balance so you can move forward once again.

Christ understood this and performed what many people of His day called "miracles." He did not believe in luck. He knew that the Infinite Power within had ability and wisdom far greater than His own and He understood how to use this Power.

"But," He pointed out, "even greater works than these shall ye do."*

Many people, however, have not learned this *Secret of Success*. They seem satisfied with themselves and their limited knowledge.

The native aborigines in Northern Australia, for example, live in a land that is rich in minerals and near a large expanse of grass for grazing which they could use to create more wealth and comfort for their people.

But they desire nothing more than food and drink and to be left alone. Even clothes are a luxury they feel they can often do without. They are satisfied with the few possessions they own and they have no serious desire to own more.

As a result of their limited desire, their lives are primitive and they have little wealth compared to those more enterprising Australians who live only a few hundred miles to the south.

* John 14: 12

In contrast, Henry Ford became rich because he thought about ways to serve more people. He started his motor company with no money of his own and found that the more people he served, the more money he earned. As the company grew larger, he re-purchased all of the outstanding shares of stock at a tremendous profit to the original investors.

Both the aborigines and Henry Ford are human beings, created in the image and likeness of God with equal opportunities around them to "accomplish all things" and prosper.

But equal opportunities are not enough. To achieve success in whatever you do, three additional things are necessary:

1. A strong desire to expand and improve everything you see and touch
2. Persistent effort until your goal is reached and
3. A continued awareness that the Infinite Spirit of Good within you is always available and willing to help you.

Your thoughts must be concentrated on ideas and plans that can create success. The words you use to express those thoughts have the power to help you create a new and better world for yourself or they can cause you to live in poverty, sickness and despair.

That is why it is so important to know and understand the words *I AM*.

I AM is the name for God. The Bible states that when Moses asked God, "What name shall I say has told me," God said unto Moses, *"I AM THAT I AM . . . this is my name forever."* *

---

* Exodus 3:14

As one of the wonderful creations of God, everything you say and do reflects your love for Him or your lack of respect. So when you say, *"I AM,"* you are actually saying, *"GOD IS."*

The right words show you love God and the wrong words or careless ones show you either do not understand his close relationship with you or you do not respect Him as your spiritual Father.

The two words, *"I AM"* have so much power they can actually create new conditions within your body and in your daily affairs.

If you say, "I am well" and repeat it several times with enough conviction, you will feel well. If you keep saying, "I am sick", you will become sick. If you say, "I am able to earn more money," God will help you secure that money. If you say, "I am poor," you will lose what you have. If you keep repeating, "I am happy," you will be happy. If you say, "I am unhappy," you will be sad.

Your choice of words, you see, can make your life much better or worse, whichever you choose. That is why you can improve your life if you will say the right words in a positive tone of voice.

"I am well.   I am strong.   I am inspired.
I am able.   I am full of love."

Repeat those words many times each day while remembering that *I AM* means *GOD IS* then you will notice some wonderful things will begin to happen in your life.

By understanding the Law of Universal Mind, which is God in Action, and cooperating with it, you can bring yourself into harmony with this Law and let It work through you and for you to bring you everything you sincerely desire.

The Truth is—there is nothing in your present environment or employment that can prevent you from rising a step or two above it.

Whatever your mind continually thinks about will grow and, eventually, it becomes a reality. That is why you, too, can accomplish greater things.

All you need to do is believe that you can do better and you will. But you must have a goal in mind. Then you must act and put your thoughts to work so that you will continuously move forward towards that goal.

Live your life with enthusiasm and *a strong desire to see what comes next.* That is the way to remain young. Children have this type of spirit.

A woman I know of eighty-nine displayed this so admirably. She always woke up with a smile and went to sleep each night with the words, "What a wonderful day tomorrow will be."

The night before she died, her friends gathered around because her doctor said she might not last till morning. They noticed a little smile in her tired eyes as she told them, "Tomorrow will be the most wonderful day of all."

When you close your eyes to the outer world (the people and things around you), you are able to enter into and know the greater world (the Kingdom of Heaven) that lies within you.

The outer world is distracting. If you allow it to gain your constant attention, you will believe it is real.

But *the Truth is*—it is not real. Every experience and every possession you have in life is only temporary and superficial.

History proves that, when such experiences and possessions are made by some mortal man, they are not perfect and cannot last.

Compared to what God has to offer, they are insignificant and of little importance. That is why philosophers say of such experiences and possessions, "These too shall pass away."

Only God and the Kingdom of Heaven He has placed within you are dependable and real. And, through His infinite wisdom and ever-present creative spirit, He can help you overcome any temporary lack of money, loneliness, physical handicap and pain.

With the help of *the Secret of Success,* you are able to rise above any circumstance and find a way to solve any problem that may exist. You can, that is, so long as you *believe* you can and have *a strong desire* to do so.

The Truth is—you are more important than you think. So do not sell yourself short. Whether you realize it or not, you are able to succeed where others fail.

Gary Player, the little 150 pound golfer from Johannesburg, South Africa, won the U.S. Open golf championship on the long and difficult Bellerive Country Club course in St. Louis, Missouri.

His victory placed his name alongside the names of Gene Sarazen and Ben Hogan as the only three men to win all four of the world's major golf trophies, the U.S. Open, the British Open, the Masters and the Professional Golfers Association tournament.

The prize for the U.S. Open was $26,000. He immediately gave away the entire amount plus another $1,000.

$25,000 went to charity and $2,000 was paid to his caddie, Frank Pagel. That was the largest sum ever known to have been paid to a caddie.

Many people can understand why a man would give away all that he earned by such hard work and concentrated effort. But there are others who cannot understand why such a man would give away an additional $1,000.

Why would he do it? Why didn't he pay his caddie

$1,000 instead of paying him the additional $1,000 which wasn't necessary?

Player said the donation of his winning check plus the $1,000 bonus was given to fulfill a promise he made to Joe Dey, the executive director of the U.S. Golf Association.

"In 1962, the U.S. Open was held at Oakmont, Pennsylvania," he said. "I wasn't rich then, but I wanted the Open championship so badly that *I promised God* that, if He gave me the privilege of winning, I would donate the entire purse to a good cause."

God did help little Gary Player to win the important U.S. Open and you may be certain that, even though he gave away $1,000 more than he made that day, he lost nothing by such a gesture.

Because he so willingly kept his promise, God will make certain that he will be repaid many times over and in many other ways.

Less than three months later, Gary Player earned $50,000 for winning the World's Series of Golf at Akron, Ohio. That amount was almost double the amount he had so freely given away.

If you should experience failure or defeat, you must realize there is no need to quit. Thousands of famous men and women and millions of others less famous failed many times before they reached their goal. They eventually found success because they kept trying with complete confidence in *the Truth* that, if one door closes, God will always open another.

Gladstone, the renowned Prime Minister of England, said, "No man ever became great or good except through many and great mistakes." That is a worthy statement to remember because too often people, who do not understand, will allow their mistakes to upset them. They look at the failure instead of learning from it.

Abraham Lincoln, for example, failed in many things. Even his marriage was not a success. He was poor, had only six months of formal schooling, had no rich friends to turn to, dressed poorly and was not as handsome as he would like to have been, yet God, in His wisdom, put him in the right place, at the right time.

He became one of our greatest Presidents because the people knew that something akin to God was present within him.

The Truth is—failure can be a blessing if you will accept it in the proper light. Mrs. Thomas A. Edison said, "Mr. Edison worked endlessly on a problem, using the method of elimination. If a person asked him whether he was discouraged because so many attempts had failed, he would say, 'No, I am not discouraged because every wrong attempt discarded is another step forward'."

F. W. Woolworth was fired by his first employer because he was "too dumb to know how to take care of the business." But Woolworth ignored that statement and continued to develop an idea for a 5 and 10 cent store.

When he started his first store, he was ridiculed by other merchants because they did not believe it was profitable to specialize in selling items at such a small price.

After his second failure, Woolworth was advised that such a business was impractical. New ideas came to him. He sensed a new power within himself and felt an increased amount of ability.

He had very little money to operate a new store, but with a determined voice he declared, "I am going to build the biggest chain of stores and the biggest building in the world." And, within a few years, he did.

Charles Ward, the late president of Brown and Bigelow, the largest company of its kind in the world, was born in poverty, sold newspapers and shined shoes in and around the saloons along the waterfront in Seattle, Washington.

After finishing high school, he left home and became a hobo riding the rails and traveling to every part of the United States.

Charles Ward associated with gamblers, smugglers, cattle thieves and fugitives from justice. He fought with the bandit, Pancho Villa, in Mexico. Finally, he was arrested for smuggling narcotics. Though he denied such an illegal activity, he was tried and convicted, and sent to Leavenworth Federal Penitentiary at the age of thirty-four.

Embittered with life, he looked for a chance to break out of prison. Then something happened within Charles Ward. He changed his attitude.

For the first time in his life, he found the answer to his problem in *the Bible*. He forgave the Federal agents who had captured him and stopped hating the judge who had sentenced him.

He resolved to create a new life and avoid the evil ways of his past. He found books in the prison library, studied them carefully and prepared himself for a job so that he would be able to pursue an honest living as soon as he was released from prison.

When Herbert H. Bigelow, president of the Brown and Bigelow company was sentenced to Leavenworth for income tax evasion, he found a friend in Charles Ward who helped him to adjust to the prison environment.

Mr. Bigelow appreciated the help he had been given. Before he left the prison, he promised Charles Ward a job in the Brown and Bigelow plant.

When Charles Ward was released, he went directly to St. Paul and was given a job as a laborer at $25 per week. But Charles Ward wanted to advance. He desired greater opportunity and more responsibility. He studied hard, learned the business and, within a year, was made superintendent of the plant. Later he became vice-president and general manager.

When Mr. Bigelow died, Charles Ward became president of the company. While president, the sales of Brown and Bigelow rose from three million dollars to over fifty million dollars per year.

Those who knew Charles Ward, during his years at Brown and Bigelow, held him in high esteem. He was trusted and loved because he helped to make this world a better place in which to live.

One of his greatest contributions to society was his employment of more than five hundred men and women who came from various prisons around the country.

The above story is interesting, but the important point to remember is—Charles Ward had a choice. He could have continued on the same difficult road with the same wrong companions and doing the same wrong things that led to failure—or—he could change his thoughts, seek a better way of life, study, prepare for an opportunity and enjoy the satisfaction that right living can bring.

Fortunately, for so many others in this world, Charles Ward chose the right road.

Albert Einstein is considered one of the greatest scientific minds the world has ever known. In school his teachers looked upon him as a shy boy, slow of speech who could rarely give the right answers to their questions and somewhat stupid.

His special talent was day-dreaming. One of his high-school teachers said, "Einstein, you will never amount to anything."

Another teacher actually suggested he leave school because his presence caused other people to want to day-dream also. Einstein gratefully accepted the suggestion and left. A year later, he was encouraged to return and laboriously finished his courses.

Although Einstein had little interest in school, he never lost his interest in science. He wanted to know what caused everything. And this eager curiosity fanned the spark that helped this one-time high school drop out to become the most famous scientist of his time.

"It is a little short of a miracle", he once said, "that modern methods of instruction have not already completely strangled the curiosity of inquiry. What the delicate life of an individual needs most, apart from initial stimulation, is freedom. For without freedom, progress is surely destroyed."

At the age of 26, while an unknown clerk in the Swiss patent office, he published his theory of relativity. Twenty years later, it was written that Einstein's theory was so difficult only ten men in the entire world were capable of understanding it.

As the years passed, scientists and physicists have used this theory to develop atomic energy and also to speed up exploration into outer space.

Lena Hemmelstein, a Russian imigrant to the United States, built the multi-million dollar Lane Bryant Company out of her idea that expectant mothers would like to have dresses that made them look less conspicuous.

The Wildroot Company was founded by two former barbers and promoted by a former driver of a junk wagon, Harry J. Lehman.

George Eastman was a bank clerk in Rochester, New York, with an idea that photography could be improved by using a "dry plate" instead of the messy wet plate then in use. His discovery of the trade name "Kodak" was due to the need he felt for an unusual name that could easily be remembered.

He accomplished this by having separate letters of the alphabet spread out before him. Then starting with A, he worked out different combinations. He was especially pleased when he reached K then O then D. KOD easily helped him finish it with A and K.

It might seem hard to make money while lying in bed, but

Robert Rhea of Colorado Springs built a successful business and earned more than a quarter-million dollars while using his bedroom for an office. His book on "The Dow Theory" was widely read by stock market technicians. He was asked to write a weekly stock market letter giving his version of what the Dow-Jones Averages indicated to him. Hundreds of wealthy investors read his letters—all written while propped up in bed.

And a hopeless cripple in Chicago earned a good living selling magazine subscriptions. He never left his room —all of the subscriptions were taken by phone.

When you have enough *faith* and *believe* in the Infinite Spirit of Good, you will find that, whatever you believe in, strongly desire, and continually persist in following, will eventually happen.

Those people whose desires are small and who believe for only a short period of time, usually fail because they lack perseverance and patience. They want results in a hurry. But it takes time for an idea to mature, just as it takes time for a flower to bloom, a tree to grow and an egg to hatch.

You must never become resigned to what unenlightened people call "fate." When you look toward *the Secret of Success,* the shadows of fear and doubt fall behind you and it is easier to help your wishes become a reality.

Most people, however, look upon a problem as a bottleneck or an unfortunate situation that is difficult to overcome. But, if you believe that your circumstances are limited, that money is scarce and people worry you, such a belief does not prove those conditions will always prevail.

They need not prevail because—with God's help, you can always improve on whatever situation you are in. And if you will lift up your chin, you can easily see the stars.

Anyone can stay in a rut because it requires no imagination or effort. But the man who has *a strong desire* to become successful will always find a way to get out.

In the remaining chapters of this book, you will learn how

you can secure more favorable results and be happy in spite of any limitation of education, finance or physical handicap you now experience.

You will be able to prove there is always a way to overcome those handicaps because handicaps are only temporary conditions. And the amount of time it takes to overcome them is shortened when you know how to "tune in" and receive more of the wisdom and power your Super-Conscious Mind is so willing to give you.

As you become accustomed to the results you receive from using your Super-Conscious Mind, you realize that nothing is too difficult for this Infinite Intelligence to solve because, being wise in all things, it already knows the answer.

When you believe in *the Secret of Success,* express enough faith and follow the leads you are given, some wonderful results can happen—and they can happen more easily.

The Truth is—whatever your conscious mind can conceive, your Super-Conscious Mind can help you achieve.

> "Life's battles don't always go
> To the stronger or faster man
> Sooner or late, the man who wins
> Is the man who thinks he can."

Mr. S. B. Fuller, a negro businessman in Chicago rose from poverty to become a millionaire. In an interview,* he said, "I left Louisiana at the age of 15 years with a sixth-grade education. My people moved to Memphis, Tennessee. At the age of 23, I hitch-hiked my way to Chicago. I got a job there and found out that I could not get ahead working for someone else.

"In 1935, during the depression, I had $25. I took the $25 and bought some soap and started selling this soap

---

* U.S. News and World Report—August 19, 1963.

from door to door. My business grew and, today, we employ more than 600 people and our sales are over $10 million per year.

"Negroes must remember that every one is born with a spark of divinity. But it's up to the individual to fan that spark. They must understand that to be successful they must own their own businesses and learn to *give* jobs—not just ask for them.

"More negroes need to learn to do as I have done. They should build up a business of their own. In Chicago, I know of a church that cost over one million dollars. Now if those people could put a million dollars in their church, they could take another million dollars and start a business. This would help them employ themselves and other people too. Furthermore, negroes must be willing to hire qualified white people just as he wants white people to hire him. In our own company, for example, 20% of our employees are white.

"Quality in an individual is developed from within. And I don't think any law can be passed that can make me any different because, in the final analysis, *I am what I think I am.*

"When I was a boy nobody helped us. You had to help yourself and you had to learn to "do." You had to have the know-how and the do-how. My mother died when I was 17. She left six besides myself. The relief people came and offered us some relief, but we did not accept it because it was a shame in those days for people to receive relief. We did not want the neighbors to know we couldn't make it for ourselves. So we youngsters made it for ourselves.

"I have a sixth-grade education, but last year (1962) I paid an income tax on over $100,000. How else could a boy with a sixth-grade education have a job in America that paid him over $100,000 a year unless he was in business for himself?"

A young man named, Charles A. Lindberg *believed* he

could fly across the Atlantic Ocean alone. Without sleep for more than 40 hours and with only a compass to guide him, he succeeded.

Walt Davis *believed* he could overcome the handicap of polio and become a high jumper. As a student at Texas A. & M. in 1954, he *believed* he could break the world's high jump record. He succeeded with a leap of 6 ft. 11½ inches.

And Dwight D. Eisenhower, as Commanding General of the Allied Armies during World War II, *believed* that the English Channel could be crossed and Europe invaded. When told that it could not be done, Eisenhower reminded his associates, "The difficult we can do right away, the impossible takes a little longer."

If you understand "the Truth that sets you free," and you *believe* that "with God's help, all things are possible," your mind will be free of tensions. You can relax and turn to *the Secret of Success* for the ideas and guidance you need. Then an answer to your problem will soon appear.

Your situation is never so bad you cannot do something to improve it—if you sincerely want to do so.

Whenever you have *a strong desire* to do better and you carry out that desire with faith in God's ability to help, then God will do whatever needs to be done to help you correct the situation or solve your problem.

Take a few minutes now to analyze your successes and failures. When you experience failure or a certain amount of unhappiness, it is primarily because you have allowed your mind to dwell on those conditions of failure or un-happiness and you have attracted them to you.

The successful man, however, has a goal in life. He has a greater desire to reach out and accomplish things and he has learned how to increase his ability by "turning up the volume" so that he can receive more of the Divine Power that is always present. He knows it is similar to turning up the volume of his radio set so that he can increase the number of stations and messages he can receive and turning carefully to the right station so he can hear the message more clearly.

Some people, however, believe only in material things. Whatever they cannot see, they refuse to understand. Yet many of those same people wonder why they are unhappy and unable to enjoy the contentment that comes from having a greater amount of *peace of mind*.

There are other people, usually humble and with limited education who have gained immortal fame because they have been willing to look for and accept this ever-dependable *Secret of Success*.

Such a man is Robert G. LeTourneau. He left school at the age of fourteen after completing the seventh grade, worked at a variety of laborious jobs and had many ups and downs. When 30 years old, he was unemployed and $5,000 in debt.

In spite of his limited education, Mr. LeTourneau has proven himself to be a remarkable inventor. Every new machine and the improved parts he has created has helped to make life easier and more pleasant for several hundred million people all over the world.

He first learned to understand *the Secret of Success* late one night in January, 1919 when his first son died. According to his book "Mover of Men and Mountains"* which I highly recommend you read, he spoke to God and said, "What have we done that we should be so punished? We've tried our best to be good Christians, where have we gone wrong?"

"The answer came, 'My child, you have been working

---

* Prentice Hall Inc, Englewood Cliffs, New Jersey

hard, but for the wrong things. You have been working for material things when you should have been working for spiritual things.'

"I had been paying only token tribute to God, going through the motions of acting like a Christian, but really serving myself and my conscience instead of serving Him.

"When a man realizes that spiritual things are worth more than material things, he will work harder for spiritual things. I had been seeking first my own way of life and I firmly believe God had to send those difficulties into the life of my wife and I to get us to look up into His face and call upon Him for His help and guidance.

"We took our problem to the Lord and felt better about it. A lot of people take their problems to the Lord, then they get up and walk away, carrying their problems with them. It is like those who pray for rain, then go out without an umbrella. If that's all the faith there is, there is not much point in praying.

"The Lord can't help you if you insist on carrying your problems with you. Leave them with Him and they are no longer your problems but His."

Mr. LeTourneau began building earth moving equipment in 1920. He started with a 5 year old tractor and a mortgage on everything he owned. In 1953, he sold his many patents and three of his five plants to the Westinghouse Air Brake Company for $31 million.

He was then at an age when most men are retired. But God kept giving Mr. LeTourneau new ideas and his active mind and body could not rest. He invented new machines and branched out into other areas. He built huge slicing machines to clear the large trees and brush from the jungles of Africa and South America, built gigantic bulldozer like machines to clear crashed bombers and other airplanes from runways, built mobil missile launchers, efficient cranes to move large logs and lumber and many others.

At the age of 76, Mr. LeTourneau, the president and chief designer of the R. G. LeTourneau Company sketches ideas for new machines and parts in chalk on his factory floor. He spends much of his 14 hour day whizzing around his plant in an electric car or bending over a drawing board, designing new equipment.

"Sometimes," he says, "I have a hard time proving to God I love Him more than my machines."

His executives ignore cost analysis, efficiency studies and other management tools. "If we can drive it out the door and it does what it's supposed to do, that's it."

In spite of this unconventional approach—and in some ways because of it—this maker of big labor-saving machines has been unusually successful.

In 1962, his company lost $1.7 million and teetered on the brink of bankruptcy. Facing lawsuits from creditors and unable to pay a $100,000 electric bill, the LeTourneau Company appeared sure to collapse.

But Mr. LeTourneau dismissed the attorney who recommended bankruptcy, stalled his creditors and finally licked the technical problems that were crippling sales. The LeTourneau Company then began to earn profits.

According to the Wall Street Journal, April 1st 1965, shares of stock in the R. G. LeTourneau Company soared, during the years 1963 to 1965, from $9 per share to $109 per share. No other stock rose as fast in the same period of time which proved that the investing public had confidence in his inventive genius and long-range judgment.

Mr. LeTourneau's limited education has never been a handicap. He wished at times he had more but, like Thomas A. Edison and Henry Ford, such a lack of formal education may have been a blessing. It enabled him and those other God-inspired men to see beyond what many more educated men said were difficult or impossible.

With absolute faith in the unfailing wisdom and creative

spirit of the Divine Mind, he says, "The Lord chooses the weak to confound the mighty" and "Every good idea I have ever had has come from God."

Because he saw so many ways he could serve more people faster and more easily, once he had the machines to do it, the ideas for making those machines have always come to him.

Mr. LeTourneau's most recent major invention is the electric wheel. It is a new way of propelling gigantic machines that makes more efficient use of horsepower because no energy is wasted on a transmission, clutch or driveshaft. "The steepest grade and the thickest mud," he said, "cannot hold it back."

Like Mr. LeTourneau, you will find that the Infinite Spirit of Good exists everywhere and in everything. Your mission on earth is to prove that is true.

Whenever you become successful, express love, bring plenty out of lack, or justice out of injustice, you prove the power of the Law of Universal Mind in Action and the wisdom of statement, "With God all things are possible."

Why was Columbus able to discover America? Educated men of his time had books that could prove the world was flat, but Columbus *believed* the world was round.

Why did Edison spend so much time on more than 20,000 experiments trying to find the right filament for the first electric light? Many educated men knew it could not be done, but Edison *believed* that, in spite of their criticism, he could find a way to cause an electric current to light up a filament inside a glass bulb.

Why did Werner Von Braun never lose faith that a rocket could eventually be built that would carry men into outer space and others could be developed to carry cameras that would take close-up pictures of the moon and Mars?

Such men never quit trying because they knew that every problem in life has a solution. They also knew that prob-

lems exist because such problems indicate there is a neces-
sity to improve on everything that men think about or do.

By concentrating your attention on whatever problem
you have, ideas will come to help you solve that problem.
This makes it easier for you to "accomplish all things."

The ideas you receive are valuable. They are God's way
of letting you know that He loves you and He wants you to
accept them. They may not be perfect because your reception to those ideas is not perfect. But you should follow
them and do as they suggest because "Faith without works is
dead."

When your faith is backed by action, new ideas will come
to help you improve on whatever you are doing. You can
then put them to work and never think of failure because
you will have the confident feeling and encouragement that
faith always gives to help you succeed.

And constant effort in the right direction will always
produce good results. That is why the right kind of practice
will lead to perfection.

If you want to play the piano, you must practice constantly in the right way or the music you produce will be
unpleasant. If you want to play football, you must learn the
right plays and practice or, as they say, "You will be
clobbered."

Only action will bring results. Wishing will not make it
so. The reason is—"God helps those who help themselves."

In the grotto at Lourdes, France, there are hundreds of
crutches crowded together that were left by people who had
been told they would never walk again.

But a visit to Lourdes gave them new hope. They had
complete faith in the power of the Divine Mind and, because
they believed this Power could heal them, they laid down
their crutches and walked.

Some came with failing sight. Many came with nervous

disorders.   Others came out of curiosity and went away
feeling a sense of increased power within.

The Truth is—everything you desire in life can be accomplished when you *sincerely believe* that it can be done.

If great men and women have become great because they
have been able to "tune in" this Infinite Mind then, obviously, you can also gain a greater measure of fame by
doing the same.

George Washington proved this at Valley Forge.   The
fortunes of the Colonists were at a low ebb.   Soldiers were
discouraged, short of ammunition, barefoot, cold, hungry
and tired.   Many had deserted.   Others were saying,
"What's the use."

It was a perfect time for Washington to quit because so
many would have agreed with him.   But Washington knew
that God would show him a way.

You know the story of how he went out from camp, knelt
beneath a tree and there, in the freezing cold and the snow,
he humbly asked God for help.

You also know that a new spirit came over the men, a new
plan of battle was arranged and from that day forward, the
tired, starving forces of General Washington went on to
eventual victory.

Was Washington great because his arms and ammunition
were plentiful or because he had well-fed troops?   No.
There was a greater power than any of those.   It was God's
plan that America become a great nation built by men who
believed in Him and freedom.

But first Washington had to ask God for help.   And that
is the way it is in your own life.   If you *desire* and ask for
what is right and proper, you will receive what you deserve,
at the right time and in the right way.   But, if you fail to ask,
you will receive little or nothing.

There is a story told about Abraham Lincoln that illustrates the importance of asking and receiving.

One day, Mr. Lincoln was driving along to court with a friend when he saw a small pig floundering around in a deep puddle of mud. Lincoln saw that the pig wanted to get out so he stepped from the carriage into the mud and pulled the pig onto solid ground.

The reason Lincoln helped that little pig out of the mud was because he could see the pig wanted to get out. But, if Lincoln had seen that pig lying there happily grunting and making no effort to get out, I am sure he would have just looked and passed on.

Yes, the Infinite Mind regards you in somewhat the same manner that Lincoln regarded that unfortunate pig. If you want help and ask for help, then the Infinite Mind will turn, immediately, like Lincoln and help you.

But, if you are content to remain as you are, even though you are deep in a puddle of problems and worries, then you will get no help because you lack the desire necessary to improve your present situation.

Since God is good, it is His nature to pour out all of the benefits you will ever need. But, in order to receive them, you must learn to relax and become aware of the good that can come to you, then gratefully accept it when it comes.

If you are at a party and the hostess offers food and drink to everyone but you keep your eyes closed or turn your head away, you cannot deny the fact she has made that offering.

Open your eyes, turn your head, be eager to receive everything the Divine Spirit has to offer.

If you do, you will receive your full share now and always.

Everything in life runs smoothly when you work with the Universal Laws of Infinite Mind that produce order and harmony. But, when you act or think in a way that is contrary to those Laws, problems arise.

The same Infinite Intelligence that keeps the stars in the

heavens, the tides of the ocean under control and the perfume in the roses is also able to guide you in every proper thing you do.

All you need to do is have *faith* in Its wisdom, ask for Its help, then *believe*—because "As you believe, so shall it be done unto you."

Since that *Truth* has been proved by thousands of believers throughout history, men and women who may have had less education and money than you now possess, it is easy to realize that, in order to be successful, all you need to do is *increase your desire, and know you can achieve it. Then with God's help,* you will be able to increase the amount of your success—more easily.

4

Thy Will Be Done

he Secret of Success never forsakes men. But men will
often forsake *the Secret of Success*.

There are millions of people all over the world who are
unhappy, discouraged, worried, frustrated or confused.
They are not sure of what course they should take. And
they miss the joy and satisfaction that comes from owning
the precious possessions of—love, happiness, peace of mind,
good health and permanent success.

The reason is—they have not learned to accept the
wisdom of the wonder-working words—

"Thy will be done."

These are the words that make it possible for you to
have *the Secret of Success* working in your favor morning, noon and night.

When problems arise and unfortunate conditions exist in
your life, think for a moment and be honest with yourself.
One of the reasons they occurred was—you put yourself
and your own wants *first*.

You turned your back on God and said, "I am going to
do it my way—not Thy way."

Such an attitude is in violation of the First Commandment which states, "Thou shalt have no other gods before
me."*

---
* Exodus 20:3

This means that any material thing or personal desire which you place first in your life or consider more important than God, is fundamentally wrong. And, because it is wrong, your road through life is difficult and you lose much of the happiness you actually seek.

The Secret of Success has arranged for your life to be continuously pleasant and happy when laudable thoughts and virtuous conduct are *continuously* followed. And, conversely, He has decreed that dishonest thoughts and improper behavior create situations that cause people to be miserable and unhappy.

"Thy will, not my will, be done" is the most dependable guideline for proper action you can ever take. By following its direction closely, you eliminate an endless number of problems and a better way of life will be opened up for you.

Too often people look in the wrong places for their help and relief. They take pep pills to pep them up and sleeping pills to help them sleep. They look for peace of mind, physical satisfaction and other pleasures in things outside themselves.

But, *the Truth is*—pep pills and tranquilizers cannot bring you peace of mind. Only a close association with *the Secret of Success* can do that.

That is why Christ said, "The Kingdom of Heaven (the infinite wisdom and creative spirit of God which is the primary element that brings permanent peace of mind, health and success) is within."

Those who listen to the Divine Spirit within them, find a new and better way of life when they carefully obey the direction of "Thy will be done."

Friendships improve, marriages are made perfect, jobs are made secure, incomes increase, crime and corruption disappear and politicians become statesmen.

And nations whose leaders say, "God's will, not my will,

be done," will be able to *understand* other nations more easily and find a way to live in harmony and peace.

If a thief would think and say, "Thy will, Father, not my will, be done," he would never commit a crime.

If a married couple would say, "Thy will, Father, not my will, be done," their marriage would be more successful and there would never be a divorce.

If an employer would say, "Thy will be done," he would find many more happy employees.

If all teen-agers would say, "Thy will, not my will, be done," there would be no teen-age delinquents.

And, if ministers all over the world would emphasize the importance of, "Thy will be done," they would find their congregations increase and a greater response to their message.

Many people, however, say, "This is the way I am and I can't help it. How can I change?"

The Truth is—you are never separated from the Infinite Spirit of God even for as long as a single breath. So, if you sincerely *desire* the greatest amount of good, you should always look *first* to *the Secret of Success*—not to places or persons whose ability to give you help or pleasure may be limited by circumstances or conditions beyond their control.

Christ asked for many things and He performed many miracles but His success came easier when he remembered to say, "Not my will, Father, but Thy will be done."

He knew that the Divine Mind to whom He spoke was wiser than He and, being wiser, It was certain to send Him the right answer to each question and the right way to carry out the answer he was given.

"With men," He said, "It is impossible, but not with God: for with God all things are possible."*

---

* Mark 10:27

You, too, will find that when you follow the direction God suggests and rely on the action He wants you to take, your life will be easier and you will enjoy more peace of mind and have greater success.

The longer you wait till you "Seek first the Kingdom of God," the longer you must wait for that peace of mind and success to become a normal part of your life.

And, of course, the more often you say, "Thy will, Father, not my will, be done," the more often you will receive the many great blessings that God is so willing to bestow.

New opportunities for advancement will then open up. And you will enjoy a richer life with a greater amount of happiness, better health and material success.

The underlying cause of all worries and problems is fear.   But, when you put your problems and worries in God's hands, how can you be afraid?

If you say, "Thy will be done" and rely on the Infinite Source of all good and allow Its creative spirit to solve those worries and problems, you will then be free from the mistakes, misunderstandings and troubles that occur when you say, "My will be done."

The reason is—God knows what is best.   He has a plan and a purpose for you and it is good—never evil or unpleasant.   It may not be clear to you what that plan or purpose is, but God knows and He wants you to carry out the ideas and suggestions He gives you.

Once you know how to work closely with the all-knowing, always dependable Infinite Mind, the answers you need will come and you will experience a great relief from tension.

So many people, however, do not believe that.   They feel that when they give more attention to God and consider *first* what He wants, they are likely to lose many of the pleasures of life.

But that is not true. God does not want you to give up anything that is either good or a permanent pleasure.

He only wants you to give up those temporary pleasures which you think are important but, actually, are of little value and can easily fade away.

Such temporary pleasures can never equal the absolutely wonderful and long-lasting peace of mind, harmony and happiness that always result from obeying the wiser attitude of "Thy will, not my will, be done."

When you allow His creative spirit to radiate through you, then you will experience a greater amount of love, prosperity, good health and success.

You will also gain the valuable virtue of patience. And, with patience, you learn how to bear all manner of unpleasant situations and conditions.

When nations meet at the conference tables, they usually leave God outside. They seldom consider what God wants. They have their own plans in mind and, even though it may take a war to accomplish their purpose, they want their plans carried out.

The result, of course, has always been disastrous because the attitude they took was based, primarily, on "my will, not Thy will, be done."

The Truth is—God will always choose those who choose Him.

Before Vonda Van Dyke became Miss America for 1965, she was asked this question, "You always carry a Bible with you. Why?"

Without hesitation, she replied, "I do not consider my Bible a good luck charm. It is the most important book I own. My relationship with God is not as a religion, but as a faith. I believe in Him. I trust in Him and hope that, even tonight, His will, will be done."

The large audience gave her a tremendous, lingering applause. When the nominations were finally made and Vonda Van Dyke was selected as the new Miss America, she cried with happiness while posing for photographers.

She told reporters, "The first thought that entered my

mind was the awful responsibility I now have to my friends, my family, my country and to my God. I will always leave my future for God's will and, winning this contest, must be part of it."

There may be times when certain events occur in your life that seem hard to bear or unfair. You may call it bad luck. You may find it necessary to take a different job, move to a new location or meet new people. But, if you continuously keep in tune with the Infinite Mind, you will find that whenever new situations are suggested to you, they will turn out, in the end, for your good.

Many people, however, do not believe in God and they have the opinion they are wise enough to run their own affairs. They try to rule other people and they will often try to force them to do things against their will.

They say, "Regardless of what you want, this is the way I want it done." But troubles and bad luck can result whenever anyone tries to force an issue or *insists* on having their way.

The Truth is—you will suffer many unpleasant experiences when you act contrary to His will.

All great men and women know that fact. That is why they are humble. They accept God's wisdom rather than denying it. They do not force their ideas or opinions on others. They have no desire to domineer. Instead, they seek cooperation and understanding.

They know that, if they *relax,* have *faith* and *believe,* God will always show them a better way.

There may be times when you say, "If only I hadn't done that," "If only I had a different job," "If only I hadn't gone to that place," etc. But happiness and peace of mind comes easily to all those who *desire the Secret of Success* and seek *first* the Kingdom of God.

On the other hand, those who do not know how to find peace of mind, will, unfortunately, turn to material things.

They call for alcoholic drinks, louder music and continuous excitement. Others turn to cigarettes and dope. Yet, after all those temporary stimulants have been tried, peace of mind still eludes them. Why?

As Christ pointed out, "With men, it is not possible, but with God all things are possible."

Yes, God can work miracles in your life and can give you many benefits and blessings but He will not give you those benefits or blessings unless you, first, are willing to let Him be the judge of what is best and right for you.

So long as you say, "I know what's best," then problems will always exist in your life and financial difficulties and unhappiness will occur from time to time.

You may never reach the point in life when you *know* everything. And that is especially true while you are comparatively young. Wisdom comes with age and knowing comes from experience. And both are enriched by understanding.

But the habit of relying more often on "God's will," rather than your will can bring you greater wisdom and understanding at a much earlier age than would be possible if God's will is seldom considered.

The child in school learns rapidly because he respects the teacher's knowledge and he listens. The young athlete improves his ability because he respects his coach who has learned from experience and he carries out the suggestions he is given. And the young scientist in the laboratory becomes proficient because he listens and learns from the professor who has learned what to do and what not to do.

Such attitudes are commendable. But you can always go one step further. You can turn, respectfully, to *the Secret of Success* and, thereby, make all of your efforts and the process of learning much easier.

If you should ever feel depressed, it is because your

conscious mind is turned in the wrong direction and you cannot recognize the blessings that your Father is so willing to give.

Without peace of mind, life seems difficult whenever you meet with adversity. With it, you have the inner strength and the moral courage that enables you to meet the challenges of life and withstand any hardship or any unfortunate circumstance that may enter your life.

God is Universal Good and He will always bring you peace of mind if you have the humility and the desire to love Him and "Seek first His Kingdom."

He does not punish you for any mistakes you make. God understands. He is always patient. And He knows that, no matter how long it takes, in time, you will learn.

You punish yourself by refusing to turn to God in time to enjoy the bounty He has to give.

The beautiful actress, Marilyn Monroe, had every material thing anyone could want—money, attraction, position, a fine home, diamonds and beautiful clothes. But she lacked the most precious possession of all—peace of mind. Failing to secure that peace of mind, she took an overdose of sleeping pills and, thus, at the early age of 34, her life was ended.

If, instead of sleeping pills, she had turned to God for peace of mind, she could have lived to enjoy the richer and more satisfying life that always seems to come to those individuals who are confident that, as they grow older, God is willing to give them more of the comforting pleasures that never fade away—but last forever.

Every day you need to make decisions. Many of them can be made quickly because experience has shown you which course to take.

But, there will be other times, when a quick decision or a right decision is difficult.

Problems will arise that may seem impossible to solve. Such cases could be a serious accident, the death of a loved one, the loss of one's business, bankruptcy or deliberate attempts on the part of others to prevent or handicap your progress.

At such times, the solution you need will always work out to your advantage if you will remember to turn to the Infinite Spirit of Good and rely on Its wisdom and judgment.

The answer will always be provided if you will sincerely have enough *faith* and *believe*.

Never try to force things. Whenever you meet with a firm resistance to whatever you want to do, it usually means that you should not continue thinking or doing anything more along that line. You had better stop for a while, go back or try some other way.

Resistance is God's way of telling you that you may not be right and you should correct it or make a change for the better.

As soon as you practice the art of understanding and cooperation, you begin to manifest wisdom and you prove that you respect God's love for all people.

But when you argue, unnecessarily, or state your position in a dictatorial way or in a domineering manner, you exhibit a limited amount of understanding.

Your mind is then closed to peaceful settlement and you cut off the free flow of good will that is so necessary if cooperation and progress are to be achieved.

If someone should say or do something to offend you, stop a minute. Before you get upset or say something that you will regret, turn to God and ask Him for help and guidance. Take time to relax before getting mad or forgive when you feel like being critical.

What other people say or do may not be right in your eyes, but your limited wisdom may fail to realize that, there may be times when their thoughts and actions may later prove to be correct.

Because that is true, it is wise to be patient, show

understanding and wait a short while before you say, "That's foolish" or "That's wrong" or "I wouldn't do it that way."

If you want people to like you, you must learn to like other people. You must give consideration to their ideas and respect their viewpoints. No matter what they might do, you must learn to overlook their mistakes and, instead, praise them for whatever they say or do that is right.

In time, your praise will encourage them to concentrate on their good points and, eventually, the improvement they make will become so noticeable that their bad points will seem only minor by comparison.

When you let God guide you and you say, "Thy will be done," you express great faith in His infinite intelligence and wisdom. Then everything in your life will fall into a more orderly pattern.

There will be times when you are right, of course, but the number of times you are right will be increased when you remember that "God works in mysterious ways His wonders to perform."

Harmony will result and you will become so confident of His love and presence that, like Christ, you can withstand all of the trials of life, overcome any sickness and lose all of your fears.

This cooperation and close association with the Infinite Spirit will give you greater strength and courage. And it will help you to resist any failure, illness or defeat that may occur.

Then, like Paul, you will be able to say, "What persecutions I endured: but out of them all the Lord delivered me.* "I have fought a good fight, I have *finished my* course and won."†

---

* 2nd Timothy 3:11
† 2nd Timothy 4:7

There is never a time in your life when you cannot make a new start or find a new opportunity. No matter what your age might be, think of yourself as being divinely guided. Then your mind will feel more at ease and nothing will upset your inner calm.

No fears or worries will trouble you because *the Secret of Success,* your Super-Conscious Mind, will furnish you with the ideas and the inspiration you need to help you overcome any adverse condition and correct every fear and fault.

You will, thereby, know for certain the benefits that result from the attitude of mind contained in the statement, "Thou will keep him in perfect peace, whose mind is stayed on Thee."[*]

You cannot change the past and you cannot live in the future. But you can enjoy the present. And the most certain way to bring success and happiness into your life today is to trust in God and know that all things are working together for your good because it is God's constant desire that all things everywhere shall be made perfect.

Cooperate with Him and say, "Thy will be done." Then your day will be blessed with a greater amount of good and your life will be moving in the beneficial stream that always flows towards perfection.

More good things will then come to you because God's way is dependable, peaceful and harmonious. And you find you no longer want to do those things which are against His will and cause your life to be filled with disorder, unhappiness and frustration.

You cannot help but benefit when you allow yourself to be guided by this Infinite Spirit of Good. All you need to do is turn to It, respect It and accept It.

Worry does not solve problems. It makes them loom

---

[*] Isaiah 26:3

larger in your mind. And it causes you to look, more often, at the problem and your own selfish interests rather than directing your attention toward the Creative Source of Good that can help you solve those problems.

God's supply of good is always available and it is not limited to any certain time or place. So when you put your problems and worries in His hands, negative and unpleasant conditions fade away because they lose their power to survive one minute after you stop thinking about them.

When you spend a few minutes with God, you increase your peace of mind. And, when you rely on Him and let His will and His Laws direct you, everything in your life tends to become easy and smooth.

Your life is then filled with all of the good things you earnestly *desire*. And you will be able to move forward in a more happy and productive way.

Christ knew that fact so well for He said, "Be not anxious," "Why are ye afraid, O ye of little faith," and "The Father within me, He doeth the work."

Those thoughts are worth remembering because nothing is ever hopeless or impossible. God is always with you and ready to help if you have *an intense desire* to reach out and *believe* that He is the creator of all good.

That is easier to do when you emphasize the words, "Thy will, Father, not my will, be done."

When things do not work out as you would like them to, do you become frustrated? When you are disappointed about something, do you get discouraged? When you have to face unpleasantness, do you get mad or upset? If so, then you are letting your will control your emotions.

As soon as you take a positive approach to what is good, *the Secret of Success* will calm your emotions and purify your reason. It will give you the inspiration, the guidance and the ability you need to succeed in all those things you *desire* which are right and honorable.

And it will be easier to do that, if you remember the words, "Peace. Be still and know that I am God."*

While that is true, many people continue to look to the wrong sources for their help.

Others try to "force" individuals around them to adopt their way of thinking. They insist that many things must be done "their way." They forget, however, that where two people or two groups are concerned, God wants each one of them to be happy and successful.

This requires that they should seek harmony, understanding and cooperation and not resort to argument, dissension and discord.

When you say, "My will be done," you are then, without realizing it, saying, "I know what is best and I am wiser than God."

But no one who is selfish or egotistical can secure the maximum amount of good because selfishness and egotism are self-defeating. They put "me first" as the important consideration and neglect "God first" which is *the Secret of Success*.

Naturally, God doesn't like such an attitude because He insists that we all follow the First Commandment.

But He is a forgiving Father. He understands our weaknesses and He will overlook your mistakes because He knows that there will be many times when you will catch yourself, reverse your position and say,

> "I'm sorry, Father, I really meant
> Thy will, not my will, be done."

---

* Psalms 46:10

5

There is No Limit to Your Potential

THERE is no limit to the wonderful things you can accomplish—if you have enough *desire,* persistent *faith* and *believe.*

That is true because—"It is your Father's wish that you shall have life and have it more abundantly."*

You have everything within you to make your life a greater success and, by turning your attention more often to God for help, you can succeed when many others fail.

If you are poor—you can always earn more money. If you are lonely—you can always create new friends. If you are ill—you can regain your health. If you are unhappy —you can enjoy more of the good things in life. And, if you are rich, you can increase your peace of mind.

To understand the reason why *the Secret of Success* is given to everyone who obeys the words, "Seek ye first the Kingdom of God," you must realize that you actually have two minds. Each one works independently. But they always cooperate with one another when necessary.

---

* John 10:10

First—you have a conscious mind that thinks, reasons, analyzes, remembers and compares. It has been given the wonderful gift of choice. And it has the ability to perceive, wonder, judge and reject. But it is limited in its wisdom. Therefore, it often makes mistakes.

Second—you have a Super-Conscious Mind. This is the all-wise, indestructible, never-failing, creative Infinite Mind which is the God-part of you Christ referred to when He said—

The Father within me, He doeth the works.*

Your Super-Conscious Mind never sleeps. It works twenty-four hours every day. It is always alert and dependable and possesses all of the wisdom and power you will ever need to help you rise above any circumstance and overcome any problem—*provided you turn to It in time and believe.*

All of the greatest scientists in the world cannot create a baby, a tree or a rosebud. Only God can create such miracles. And He creates them easily and with reliability over and over again—many millions of times each year.

The Truth is—your conscious mind does not have the power nor the ability to create anything. It can only *make use of* the many elements which God has created.

Your conscious mind does this under the direction of your Super-Conscious Mind just as a construction worker follows the direction of his foreman. So long as the worker carries out the plans he is given, the work he is doing will be completed properly and on time. But, if that worker should say to himself, "I believe I will do this my way," then problems can arise and the job may have to be corrected or done over.

---

* John 14:10

That is why that worker will always find it wiser to say, "Thy will, not my will, be done."

When you allow your conscious mind to "think for itself," it will often make mistakes because its ability is limited to what it can learn from worldly experience or from other people such as teachers, friends, neighbors and parents whose minds are also mortal and limited.

The ideas you receive and the creative ability you possess comes from your Super-Conscious Mind or is relayed to you from someone else who has received it from this Super-Conscious Mind.

This Mind is the vital, constantly expansive Creative Spirit that has enabled mankind to progress from cave man to astronaut and have all of the comforts we now enjoy.

Without Its help, we would still be living in caves and wearing bearskins.

Your Super-Conscious Mind works faithfully and tirelessly whether you are awake or asleep—even under the influence of an anesthetic. It governs all of the involuntary processes of your body such as digestion, elimination, the beating of your heart, the circulation of your blood, the growth of your skin, hair, nails, etc. All in perfect order without your conscious mind having to think about such a phenomenon.

It can build every cell of your body, diagnose and cure disease, create ideas, solve problems and convey all sorts of knowledge which, at this moment, may be unknown to your conscious mind.

It has no desires nor volition of Its own. It has Infinite knowledge and powers. It acts in response to suggestions given to It by your conscious mind and It works to bring about the exact condition you believe in.

The Truth is—you are never alone. This all-wise Super-Conscious Mind, which is God, is always with you. And the only thing that will ever prevent you from gaining all of the benefits and good luck you would like to have is your unwillingness to turn to It in time.

But, if you should fail to keep "in tune" with this Infinite Creative Mind, then you alone are responsible for the pleasures and the opportunities you will miss.

That is what is meant by the statement, "You are master of your fate and the captain of your soul."

Many people know that fact but they ignore it. They have not learned how to work in harmony with *the Secret of Success* which is—"Seek ye first the Kingdom of God and His righteousness; and all good things shall be added unto you."

That is the reason why, when you look around, you will find that all of the confusion, the misunderstandings and the unpleasantness in the world are man made.

Most of the things in nature, however, are harmonious. And, when harmony exists, all things are beautiful, peaceful and happy.

The mighty tides of the ocean ebb and flow twice each day in perfect rhythm and harmony. The stars and planets race through space at terrific speeds, yet they are always in their proper place.

Why is that true? Why do so many things in nature live harmoniously and successfully while man will so often experience confusion, anxiety, tension and fear?

Why can't man always enjoy the same poise, serenity and peace that everything else in the Universe enjoys?

The answer is—nature is more harmonious than man because it accepts the wisdom and power of the Infinite Intelligence that guides all things. It has *a desire* to expand and grow. And it cooperates with this Creative Spirit because it *knows* and *believes* that every good need will be met.

It does not worry needlessly about tomorrow because it

has *faith* and *believes* that, if *the Secret of Success* is considered and allowed to guide and develop everything, tomorrow will always be better than today.

It is grateful for all the good it is given then expresses its thanks by doing something that will make some other thing in nature more happy.

Man, on the other hand, does not enjoy the same amount of harmony because he turns his mind away from God so many times each day. In a sort of egotistical way, he believes that he can make continuous progress without being in touch with the Infinite Source of all good.

That is the reason why so many people fail—while others succeed. That is the reason why so many people are unhappy—while others have friends and know the joy of living. And that is the reason why so many people blame luck or someone else for their ill fortune—while others thank God for all the good things they experience.

The Truth is—your success or failure is due to the attitude you have towards life and the way you think and believe.

To achieve a lasting and dependable amount of success, you must "Seek *first* the Kingdom of God." And you must have a *desire* to do something rather than nothing.

Then you must develop a plan or a purpose. You must know where you are going and what you are going to do when you get there.

Without a plan or a purpose, confusion can result. Then you eventually become unhappy and your loss of interest will cause you to fail in whatever you do.

When your desires are clearly defined and you think positive thoughts and take positive action, you can accomplish anything you *desire* and *believe* you can do.

But, if you drift along without a goal, if you have no clearly defined purpose, or if you lack the *desire* to succeed, then, like the cork bobbing up and down on the ocean, you allow yourself to become a victim of circumstances. You will be a "slave" to the will of others rather than "master of your own soul."

The direction your conscious mind takes is important. That is why you should "Seek *first* the Kingdom of God" and always say, "Thy will, not my will, be done."

The reason is—whatever you think about, whatever you feel and every word you speak is impressed on your Super-Conscious Mind.

Your Super-Conscious Mind then sets out to cause whatever you think about and whatever you feel to come into being. In other words, you eventually get what you ask for.

Since that is true, you can see why all of the conditions you experience, whether they be good or bad, are the result of the way you have thought, felt or spoken.

Therefore, the only way you can prevent unhappiness, sickness and lack of money to enter your life is to replace those negative thoughts with more positive thoughts that will direct your life towards happiness, health and wealth.

You can understand this better when you realize that your Super-Conscious Mind is like a tape-recording machine. Whatever you say, whatever impression you want to create and every moment of hesitation you make is carefully recorded on the tape.

When the tape is played back, you will find that the recorder has faithfully recorded every word and every inflection of your voice *exactly* as you gave it.

If you spoke positive words in a positive tone of voice, the recorder will play back positive words in a positive tone of voice. If your words contained negative thoughts, moments of hesitation or indicated a weak tone of voice, then that is *exactly* what will be reproduced.

When it is finished, you do not blame the tape recorder for any mistakes you hear. You never say, "That isn't me. I

spoke positive words and it reproduced negative ones."
You accept the accuracy of the recording.

But the words and thoughts you have expressed can
always be changed or improved. By turning on the switch
marked "record," the tape recorder can be re-run. All of
your previous words can be "erased" and new words and
thoughts can be impressed on the tape to produce a more
pleasant result.

So, if you are not satisfied with the way your affairs are
working out, you can improve them by "erasing" all of the
old, negative, self-defeating thoughts and "recording" new
and more positive thoughts on your Super-Conscious
Mind.

Your Super-Conscious Mind will then set out to make
certain that whatever new desires you have impressed upon
it will eventually come to pass. In this way, you can create a
new way of life that will be more in line with the way you
want it to be.

That is the meaning of the statement, "As you
believe—so shall it be done unto you."*

Some people wonder, however, why their life does not
run smoothly.

When you take the time to analyze their thoughts and the
words they speak, you will find that most of their thoughts
are negative and they like to complain about their troubles.
The result is, they always have some troubles to complain
about.

Other people find life is more agreeable. They feel that
any difficulty they face is only temporary and most of the
situations they experience each day will result in happy
endings.

These facts are true because the words and thoughts you

---

* Matthew 8:13

express have a tremendous vibratory power. They can create pleasant situations in your life or unpleasant ones according to the way you express them.

So you see, by changing your thoughts and the words you speak, you can change your life from good to bad or from bad to good and cause it to become anything you wish.

You alone can do this—no one else can do it for you.

That is why your life can always be improved. And it is the reason why every unpleasant feeling and illness you experience is the result of some mental or spiritual upset.

The negative thoughts of fear, hate, anger, jealousy and resentment create negative conditions within your body. Doctors of psychosomatic medicine say they will produce headaches, nausea, neuralgia, constipation and backaches. And the continuous expression of such negative thoughts will produce stomach, liver and heart troubles.

The only permanent basis for health and happiness is to make certain that your mind is free of confusion and your attention is focused on God-inspired thoughts that will create both health and happiness. In this way, you can have a greater amount of mental and spiritual harmony in your life.

To prove how the thoughts you express can create unpleasant conditions in your life, or unpleasant ones, according to the way they are expressed, all you need to do is say these words slowly and emphatically three times.

"I feel sick and tired. I am broke. Everything has gone wrong. Nobody loves me. The whole world is in a pitiful mess."

Have you said them three times? Notice how bad you feel. In just one minute, you have made yourself feel miserable. Naturally, you can see that, if you *believe* those words and repeat them often enough each day (as so many people unfortunately do) you will certainly feel bad and nobody should be blamed but yourself because you are the one who thought them.

Now say the following words three times in a positive, emphatic tone and notice the difference.

"I feel wonderful and full of pep. I see plenty of money coming to me. Everything is running smooth. Everybody likes me. I know this is a wonderful world full of wonderful people and I know some wonderful things will happen to me today."

Have you said them three times in an enthusiastic tone? Now you feel much better don't you.

With practice, you will find you can change and improve your thoughts just as easily as you can change and improve the programs on your radio or television set. With a little effort, you can tune in any station you desire and you can switch from programs that show crime, violence or unhappiness to other programs that are more pleasant.

And, with the same amount of effort, you can tune in and receive messages of help from your Infinite Super-Conscious Mind and you can change the conditions under which you live or improve your environment.

So all you need to do when you *desire* success is to change whatever negative, soul-destroying thoughts you may have to positive, creative thoughts and spend more time thinking of the better conditions and experiences you want to happen in your life.

Furthermore, you must never give up. Many wonderful things will come to you—more easily—if you have enough faith and will continue to believe.

Fleet Admiral Chester W. Nimitz said, "God grant me the courage to not give up on what I believe is right—even though I might think it is hopeless."

6

How to Tune in the Infinite Mind

WHEN you accept the fact that there is an all-knowing, all-powerful Infinite Mind called God, it explains the "miracles," the "cures" and the mysterious phenomona that, for thousands of years, have mystified a scoffing and half-believing world.

Since God possesses infinite wisdom and His creative spirit is always available, it is obvious that you can increase the amount of your success by appealing to Him for help.

No matter what your problem or difficulty may be, when you are in trouble or need an answer to your problem, He will always help you find that answer. All you need to do is ask.

That is simple logic. But, like so many other things we know about, we often take it for granted and fail to ask Him in time.

It is like the business man who was bankrupt. His brother visited him and, during the visit, the business man lost his temper. "Why didn't you help me?," he said, "Then I wouldn't be in this fix."

"Because you never asked me," replied his brother.

Much of the success you seek will come if you make

certain to ask in time. That is why it is so important to turn to the Infinite Mind before your troubles start—before your problems get too deep.

When you know how to "tune in" the Infinite Mind, you can make yourself the happy, successful person you want to be.

Too often, men and women are inclined to say, "I can figure this out myself," "I can beat it," or "I'm going to do it my way."

But there is an easier, more reliable way. It lies in the belief and constant practice of the statement, *"Thy will, Father, not my will be done."*

When you turn your attention towards *the Secret of Success,* you will receive ideas and directions that will help you to solve your problems and they will encourage you to eliminate any difficulty under which you may labor. As a result, you will have greater *peace of mind* and financial security will come more easily.

Sometimes the answer to your question, "What shall I do," may not seem logical.

It may tell you to give up something you want, leave a residence you love or give up a job you feel is important.

But resisting or saying "No" is not the way to carry out the suggestions you receive from your Super-Conscious Mind. This is especially true if, by resisting or saying "No," the problem or unfortunate situation remains.

Your Super-Conscious Mind—the God Mind within you—knows everything. It is perfect. And it will work with you at all times to help you. But you must be willing to cooperate with It and know how to keep in constant contact with Its infinite power.

Whatever you wish for and whatever you *desire* will always come to pass if it is God's will. When you know and believe your *desire* is right, hold it firmly and constantly in your mind. Then ask *the Secret of Success* for the ideas and ways to follow and It will help you secure that desire.

Your best ideas and solutions to problems will come when you are completely relaxed and quiet. Many of them will come while you are alone or sitting in darkness. Others will come while you are asleep.

That fact proves that the ideas you receive come from a dependable, ever-helpful Super-Conscious Mind that works through your conscious mind and It gives you those ideas, freely, because you are relaxed and receptive.

You will find it is easy to secure new ideas and improve on your old ideas. And you will be able to accomplish more things with less effort and without strain. By using Its greater wisdom, you will have the answers you need whenever you *desire* to make a wise decision.

If you have never played a piano nor tried to hit a golf ball straight down the fairway, you might think they are difficult. But, when you learn the knack of how a piano should be played and how to hit a golf ball straight and true, then you can, with practice, do as well as most everyone else.

Whenever you learn how to tune in the Infinite Super-Conscious Mind, you will be able to create the conditions that will enable you to live a more enjoyable life. You will be able to attract the ideal business partner, the right mate and the right situations that will bring you all of the abundance, security and peace of mind you will ever need.

There may be times when adverse thoughts of fear and doubt may enter your conscious mind. You may think or say, "It can't be done," "I don't believe it" or "Some people can do it, but not me." But all of such negative thoughts will eventually cause you to experience unpleasant conditions.

By thinking and saying such thoughts, you are in effect saying, "God cannot help me" when *the Truth is—*

The infinite wisdom and creative spirit of
God will always supply you with ideas and
encourage you when all other ways and other
people fail.

All you need to do is *relax,* have enough
faith to listen to Its wisdom and *believe* what
you hear.

There is no limit to what the Infinite Mind can do for you.
The only limitation is in the amount of contact you have
with this Infinite Mind.

If you contact It very little, It will produce very little for
you. If you contact It constantly and turn to It with *faith*
and *belief,* It can produce conditions and events in your life
that many people may regard as "miracles."

Think of the miracle of being in a dark room, yet with the
flick of a switch, the universal energy that is always present
in that room can be captured in a small glass bulb and
"presto" light appears.

Thomas A. Edison produced that miracle. And think of
being able to capture a person's voice, press it on a piece of
wax and play it over and over again for many years. Edison
accomplished that miracle also.

"The ideas behind those miracles," Edison said, "Just
dawned on me." He realized and never doubted that they
came from God.

And Luther Burbank, the botanist who performed so
many miracles with fruits and flowers said of the ideas he
received, "They seem to come to me from out of the air."

The Truth is—Edison, Burbank and every other great
believer in *the Truth,* knew that all of the ideas that have
ever existed or ever will exist and all of the answers to every
problem in life have always been known by the Infinite
Mind.

If Thomas Edison had not invented the electric light, someone else, sooner or later, would have discovered it. The idea had been floating around in space for thousands of years. Edison had the *desire* to create it and "tuned in" before anyone else.

At this very moment, you have the same ability as Thomas Edison to charge yourself with the spiritual energy to accomplish anything you sincerely *desire*. You have every opportunity to receive all of the ideas and inspirations available to such enlightened men as Shakespeare, Emerson, Lincoln, Mozart and Ford, if they were alive today.

All of this power is available for you to use now, at any time and without any limit. It is available to you with little effort. All you have to do is recognize the Source from which it comes, turn to It then *"Ask and believe and you shall receive."*

Let us assume that the radio in your home is now turned off. You hear nothing. But you know there is music, drama, news and information striking that radio at this very moment.

Because you hear nothing does not prove that no news nor music is there. If you turn on your radio and tune in a station, it gives out freely.

Your Super-Conscious Mind is like your radio. If you turn off the contact between your conscious mind and your Super-Conscious Mind, so that ideas, information and answers to your problems cannot come through. Then, of course, like your radio that is turned off, you will not receive those ideas. But, if you "tune in" the unlimited power of Infinite Mind and allow your conscious mind to receive the ideas, directions and messages it is sending out, they can help you solve all of your problems and point out the way to furnish all of your needs.

You can only hear the news on your radio by being in

tune with the station. And God can only help you by being in tune with His Infinite Mind and the wisdom He has to offer.

That is why it is so necessary to be receptive. If you are constantly in tune with the Infinite Mind, amazing things will happen. Your family and friends may even call them "miracles."

Suppose that a radio station were to announce your name and say that you were entitled to a prize of $10,000. To win, all you needed to do was tune in the station and hear your name announced. If your radio was not tuned to that station, you would never receive that prize no matter how many times they announced it.

Like the radio station above, the all-wise, ever-helpful Infinite Mind has many prizes to offer. According to the United States Patent Office, it offered 1,083 to Thomas A. Edison.

More are being offered every minute of the day. They are yours for the asking—"no strings attached." The only requirement is—*you must be tuned in and receptive.*

Here is how you can tune in the Infinite Mind and receive all the good things It has to offer.

First—you must have faith and believe this Infinite Mind exists. Then relax completely.

This means that you must find a quiet place where you will not be disturbed by outside noises nor by other people. No problems of importance and no worries can easily be solved until you first have *faith* and then *relax*.

Flowers, trees, birds and animals all have this *faith*. They also know how to *relax*. And, as Christ pointed out, "Are ye not much better than they."*

Their *faith* allows them to grow, produce and reproduce

---

* Matthew 6:26

easily and naturally without any strain nor worry about tomorrow.

Second—if you have a problem to solve, do not try to make God understand. Give Him credit for superior wisdom and knowledge. He already knows the answer and, at the right time, He will give you that answer.

Do not explain to God how your problem should be solved nor tell Him how a certain decision should be made. That is the hard way. It is not effective because, first, it is selfish on your part. It assumes "my way be done," not "Thy will be done." Second, it assumes that your wisdom and knowledge is greater than God's.

Try the easy way. Let God know about your problem, then *relax* and say, "Not the way I want it, but Thy will (the way You want it) be done."

Have *faith* that, while you may have some ideas of your own on how to solve your problem or how you would like it to turn out to be, the Infinite Mind will give you a better answer and show you a better way.

As a matter of fact you will be surprised to find out how many times the way you thought would be the best way will turn out to be unsound.

There will also be times when you will receive no answer at all.

The reason is—you may feel that your problem must be solved immediately or in a way you personally like but God may prefer that your problem should be worked out in a way that is different from the way you might want.

His way may even be contrary to what you had in mind. But "Thy will be done" is still wiser and more certain of success than "my will be done."

Finally—in order to have complete success, you must not worry, wonder nor "try" in a way that is tense or strained.

You must have complete *faith* and *believe* that the power

and wisdom of the Supreme Intelligence is always ready and willing to help you in every way.

Christ said you must "Enter into thy closet and shut thy door."*

If you should be tense, confused and worried, you will find it easier to relax if you will lie down on a couch or a bed, lean back in a chair or put your feet up on a desk.

Then place your thumbs on your temple and the fingers of each hand in the center of your forehead and say to yourself—"peace." Hold your fingers there and repeat the word "peace" several times every few seconds.

When you feel completely relaxed and at ease, then place the tips of your ten fingers together and either put your hands loosely in your lap or place them in front of your chest.

The wise men of every age have found that this prevents the spiritual energy within your body from escaping. It keeps this energy circulating within your body and enables you to increase your inner power so that you can more easily "tune in" the broadcasting station which is God.

Then shut your eyes and allow your mind to turn *inward—not outward.* Christ said, "The Father within me, He doeth the work."

There is a gland in the center of your brain called the pineal gland. Ancient philosophers called it "the third eye," and "the all-seeing eye."

It is now believed by metaphysicians that the pineal gland is the spot in your brain where messages are received from the Infinite Intelligence. So, when you turn your thoughts "inward" and focus them on the pineal gland in the center of your brain, it is easier to receive the answers to all of your problems and your desires.

---

* Matthew 6:6

To be successful and get the maximum results, you must *relax*. And the more relaxed you are, the more successful your results will be.

You must let go of your worries, doubts or fears. That is what is meant by the statement, "Be still and know that I am God."

A relaxed state of mind is important. If you ask God for help, you must be willing to allow Him the freedom to help you in the way He knows is best.

Whenever you try to force your will or your ideas into solving your problem or securing what you want, the results you seek will not be as easy nor as successful as allowing the Infinite Mind to send you the answers that can more easily solve those problems.

That is true because anything that is "forced" or "ill-got" will always show unfortunate results.

You must, at all times, have absolute *faith* that God has the right answer to your problem.

Do not wonder if this is so. "God works in mysterious ways, His wonders to perform."

Know that is true and you will find a new poise and power surging through your entire being.

Believe it and you will find that anything you attempt will become easier.

7

The Law of Evolution

AND the Lord said, "Behold I make all things new."* When you allow your mind to dwell too long on things of the past, you miss out on much of life's progress. What happened yesterday is not as important as the good things that can happen tomorrow.

The fundamental purpose of all life is to grow, expand and progress. Success, therefore, is more certain when you focus your attention and your talents on those matters in your life that can eventually bring about such growth, expansion and progress.

So many people long for "the good old days." But they lose sight of the fact that, while our present world is not perfect and can be improved, it is better than anything we have known in the past.

Now is the most important, exciting and promising time of your life.

Nothing in life was meant to be static. Growth and change are normal and necessary to progress. That is why everything that exists can be improved or changed into something that can be used to help bring about God's ultimate goal of perfection.

Those people who like to be regarded as open-minded

---

* Revelations 21:5

and intelligent look to the future with eager expectation. They are confident that our human nature is evolving higher and higher. They believe that the majority of those who live in the present generation are better than those of the past and, with God's help, the majority of those who live in the next generation will be even better than the present.

Many people used to laugh at any new thought or idea. Now we are wiser. Nobody dares to laugh today, because we know that tomorrow the new thought or idea that was expressed may someday come true.

Research, for example, never reaches a conclusion. It increases knowledge, opens up new possibilities and discovers new things that are, at present, unknown.

Progress is made through trial and error and a thousand men may try and be wrong before one may try and be right.

Those who failed should never be ridiculed. Such men are necessary if progress is to be made. Instead, they should be praised and encouraged for trying. Otherwise, their adventurous spirit would be crushed and the great and continuing desire of men to get up and grow would no longer be present within them.

What would life be like today if someone had said "No" to Columbus and refused to allow him to sail? What if someone had said, "Don't do it," to Benjamin Franklin, "you might kill yourself," when he flew his kite, coaxed the lightning down his kite and discovered the principle of electricity? What if someone had convinced the Wright Brothers to stay on the ground where it was safe?

What if no one had faith in Henry Ford and refused to invest the money necessary to build his cars? What if someone had prevented the first doctor form using pain-relieving anesthetics for fear they might kill his patient? What if someone had discouraged Marconi against experimenting in wireless transmission or said, "It's a waste of time" to P. T.

Farnsworth when he was trying to produce pictures from out of the air?

What if D. D. Palmer had not modernized the healing arts by discovering the principle and philosophy of chiropractic?

Where would civilization be today if such men did not obey this *Law of Evolution?*

That is why the spirit of adventure and the willingness to invest both time and money must be encouraged. And those who make an effort should not be penalized unfairly should they happen to fail.

Ideas were given to men and they were developed because God gives men the *desire* to create. And He gives them *a desire* to know, *a desire* to do and *a desire* to never be satisfied with things as they are but to experiment and try to find new and better ways to improve things.

A business, for example, that wants to grow and earn more money must find new ideas, new products, and new ways of serving more people. Then it must hire more people with new ideas to create more products to serve more people and continue to follow that program so long as it is possible.

The Truth is—God never intended that this world should be a resting place. It is actually a testing place. He wants you to grow in spite of the troubles and difficulties you experience.

That, in brief, is the true nature and purpose of your existence.

The moment you find nothing more to strive for and work towards, you start a decline towards mediocrity.

Then life becomes a bore and, as a person, you begin to fade away from a somebody to a nobody.

Many people wish that life would be easy and smooth-sailing, full of comfort and no pain, all vacation and no work, everything perfect without any struggle. But such a life would not be pleasant for long.

You can escape the hardships of life only by giving up the adventures.

The Truth is—adversity, troubles and problems can be a blessing if you look at them in the proper light. They are the seed of opportunity. That is why the Hindu philosophers say, "Whenever one door closes, God opens another."

New opportunities are opening up all over the world due to the new inventions, better communications and better transportation that were not available to you yesterday.

To be successful and grow, you must continually try something new. Have a desire for adventure. Focus your thoughts on the good and wonderful things that can happen in the future. And fill your mind with eager expectation. It will help to keep you young and vital.

Do something different and you will find life more interesting. Dream a little. Plan to take a trip. Meet new people. Read new magazines and books. Attend a different church. Find a new restaurant. Get out of your every-day routine for awhile and you may learn something of value you can use at a later date.

David Sarnoff, Chairman of the Board, Radio Corporation of America, pointed out that, "Whatever course today's youths have chosen for themselves, it will not be a chore but an adventure if they bring to it a sense of the glory of constantly striving—if their sights are set far above the merely secure and mediocre. In one's personal life, as in world affairs, appeasement, the easy way out and the lack of effort can be the shortest road to failure and defeat."

And Rosalind Russell, the distinguished actress, said, "To learn to live with failure and then overcome it has contributed more to the success I have known than any other factor."

To keep *the Secret of Success* working in your favor, you must focus your thoughts and desires on the future.

The reason is—you must obey a fundamental Law of Universal Mind called—*the Law of Evolution.**

This Law, like all of the other Laws in this book is Spiritual. It was made by God. Therefore mortal men, whose ability to reason is imperfect—as compared to God— should not, in any way, act contrary to Its wisdom. To do so may result in days of hardship, heartache, and oftentimes, financial loss.

When you understand this *Law of Evolution,* you will know the reasons why so many people are happy and successful and why so many others are unhappy and unsuccessful.

There is no fun nor pride in staying in a rut. The fun and pride comes from raising your sights and setting all of your goals a little higher.

When you become satisfied with yourself and the progress you have made, you cut yourself off from *the Secret of Success.*

But striving to improve everything you do requires time, some effort and sacrifice. The rewards, however, are great. They give you pride of self-accomplishment. They increase your confidence. They cause people to respect you and they will often lead to greater income from your work.

The Law of Evolution means that, whenever the Infinite Intelligence inspires you to believe that the thoughts and plans you are given will help you to serve more people, you must continually move forward in everything you do. You must not allow anything nor anyone to cause you to "stay as you are" or "to go backwards."

A tree follows this *Law of Evolution* when it grows around the rock that tries to smother its growth. The

---

* Note:—This *Law of Evolution* should not be confused with the *theory of evolution* which is an assumption by some who do not believe in the infinite wisdom and creative power of God. They are inclined to believe that man may have evolved from monkeys and earlier in history may have evolved from miniature life in the sea.

mountain stream proves this Law when it flows over and around any obstacle in its way. And man proves this *Law of Evolution* by the progress he makes.

You will find that there is always a better way to do things. And *the Law of Evolution* requires that you find that way.

When you drive an automobile, you know you cannot move forward successfully with the brakes on. At least it is difficult to do so. The friction is too great.

Many people say they want better health, more money, more love, and a chance for self-expression. But a simple want is not enough. It will not create as much of those things as *a strong desire*.

Life is improved when you release the brakes of negative thoughts that can hold you back and allow your desire to increase so you can think positive thoughts that will help you to move forward more easily and naturally.

"The world hates change," Charles F. Kettering said, "yet change is the only thing that has brought progress."

Some people regard change as unnecessary. Others look upon change with fear and foreboding. Paul, however, in Romans 12:2 wrote, "Be not conformed to this world, but be ye transformed by the renewing of your mind, that ye may prove that good, and acceptable and perfect will of God."

Those who believe in *the Secret of Success* and *the Law of Evolution* welcome constructive change because it helps to bring about God's plan to improve and perfect all things. As such changes occur, so do opinions and attitudes. The statement, "This is the best way. Why change?" is overcome, in time, by the statement, "This is a better way. Let's do it."

Most of the men and women of the past six thousand years, who were successful, actually started with a handicap. They made progress because they had a feeling that inspired them to *believe* that, in spite of their handicap, there was a greater power and wisdom than their own which they could use to help them succeed.

Miracles happened because they *believed* in miracles. Wondrous things happened because they *believed* in wondrous things. Happiness, money and fame came to them because they *believed* that happiness, money and fame were possible.

They had *a strong desire* to do better and they went to work and did it.

They were obeying this *Law of Evolution* which requires that you constantly improve yourself and have *an intense desire* to add to your present knowledge—to grow and expand your present field of activities.

When you enthusiastically follow this *Law of Evolution*, you rise above mediocrity. You no longer feel bored or discouraged. You eliminate "the blues" and the depressed feelings that often occur. And you find that, the higher you rise in spirit, the greater your interest in life becomes and the more interesting things you will see.

Abraham Lincoln proved this *Law of Evolution*. As a young man living in poverty and without any outside stimulation, he could sense that something better lay ahead for he said, "I will study and prepare myself, and someday my time will come."

If you want to reach your goal, you must guard against discouragement. You cannot afford to give up too soon. You only fail when you quit and you are only defeated when you admit that you can't.

You only limit yourself by limiting your vision.

The world needs more people who can inspire others and encourage them to "Arise, take up thy bed and walk."

The Truth is—anyone can fail because it takes no effort. The day before Columbus discovered the shores of America his sailors threatened to mutiny. They wanted to turn the ship around and go home.

Dr. Paul Ehrlich, the great German bacteriologist, sought an effective treatment for syphilis. He prepared an arsenical compound called salvorsan. He named it "606" because none of the 605 other compounds he tried could overcome the disease.

And Edison tried over twenty thousand experiments before he found the right filament for his electric light.

Every time you feel discouraged, turn immediately to *the Secret of Success* for help. Say to yourself, "I know that, with God's help, I can do it. The ideas I need will come and the leads He gives me I will follow."

If you have enough patience and *believe* in His love and willingness to help you, ideas will arise in your mind that will enable you to solve whatever problem you may have— provided you act and follow through on the hunch or lead you are given.

An intense *desire* to achieve—to do something rather than nothing—is a feeling that is vitally important if you want to be successful.

Desire is creative power. It is God's way of saying, "Progress. Move up higher." It is the motivating force that helps you rise up and do better—to carry out God's plans to develop and perfect this world.

The two-year-old child exhibits this *desire* when he insists on dressing himself or tying his own shoes. The ten-year-old daughter exhibits this *desire* when she wants to bake a cake or make some fudge. The teen-ager wants to win a game and the college student who is ambitious wants to create a better world or build an empire when he graduates.

Failure to move ahead or expand will often lead to frustration and unhappiness. A tree grows because it has a *desire* to grow. If it did not, it would be stunted and ugly.

A river has a *desire* to reach the sea. If it did not, it would become dirty and full of scum. A flower blossoms because it has a *desire* to proclaim, "Thank you God for the beauty You have placed within me."

I have talked with men who have not had a new idea in 20 years. They are mentally and spiritually in a rut. They miss many of the blessings that are available because they are reluctant to try something new.

Progress goes on but they fight it as though such progress was wrong and unnecessary. They will not accept it unless it has first been made perfect.

They fail to realize that, new ideas and progress are fundamentally good and perfection comes only through practice, trial and error and eliminating what is not needed while keeping that which is productive and worthwhile.

The negative state of mind, the doubting habit, will do more than anything else to keep you from getting what you want out of life. When you doubt, you fail. And, when you fear, you may become ill. When you hold back, you are unable to move forward and your whole life is then lived in violation of this *Law of Evolution.*

Because you have "the Kingdom of Heaven within you" —the wonderful power and infinite wisdom of God—you have an unlimited capacity for growth. And you can always unfold into someone who is wiser, finer and better.

But, in order to achieve the many great things that are possible, you must work closely with *The Secret of Success* and replace your negative thoughts with positive, constructive thoughts.

You must do this no matter how hard it may seem. The longer you put it off, the longer you say, "It can't be done" or "I don't have a chance," the longer it will take to improve the conditions in your life.

Instead of moaning and feeling inadequate, you must stir yourself inside so that you have *a strong desire* to improve and move ahead.

Then you will feel more confident because you will be looking up and *believing*. And the progress you seek will be easier.

As you grow older, too many negative opinions may be offered by friends, relatives and associates who might say, "It can't be done," "Why try, you'll never make it" or "What's the use, there's too much competition." But those who express such negative thoughts forget four important points:

1. There is plenty of room at the top because so many people are content to remain near the bottom.

2. Those who try are always noticed.

3. The Lord helps those who help themselves and

4. To be defeated, but never quit is the mark of a man who is destined to become a success.

There is nothing to equal the contentment that comes from producing and growing. But growth and progress takes time and effort. That is why it is so important to follow a plan that will help this *Law of Evolution* work in your favor.

Time proves many things—especially the wisdom of God's will (not thy will) be done. When you feel like giving up, turn more often to *the Secret of Success* for help. Ask Its creative wisdom for guidance. If you listen carefully and humbly, your Super-Conscious Mind will tell you one of two things:

> "Yes, you should give up because you are on the wrong road."

> or

> "Keep trying. Tomorrow will be a better day."

Whichever suggestion you receive, follow it. Don't argue with it. No matter what your limited wisdom may think, the way that God points out will always prove to be the best.

Distractions can often be detours on your road to success. Many men have learned that, in order to make progress, they have had to say, "No, thank you" to their friends who have suggested going to a dance, playing golf, cards or any other game. They have had to leave a room to avoid seeing a television program. And some have had to ignore the ringing of their phone to prevent being disturbed.

The difference between failure and success lies in changing the words, "I can't" to "I can."

When you say, "I can't," you set up negative vibrations in your mind that work like a brake against this *Law of Evolution*. They make it difficult to succeed.

On the other hand, when you say, "I can," you set up positive vibrations that enable you to succeed where others fail.

"I can't afford it" and "I can't do it" are two more negative phrases that will always make your life more difficult and unpleasant. They create conditions that will eventually lead to some form of poverty and failure.

If you constantly say, "I can't afford it" or "I can't do it," then you alone will be responsible for the poverty or failure that will always result from such a negative attitude.

But when you consistently say "I know I can do it if I try," you set up positive vibrations that help your life proceed more smoothly because they work in harmony with this *Law of Evolution*.

1. Start in a small way but make every effort to secure a position in a business or a profession that interests you. For with interest comes love and love creates happi-

ness. That is why if you are interested in what you are doing, you will be happy.

2. Let people know what you can do, then ask them to allow you to do it.

3. Write down a specific goal then make every effort to reach it.

4. Take the time necessary each day to study, prepare and practice so that each new effort shall be better than the last.

5. When a certain goal is reached, set a new goal just a little higher. The minute you stop moving forward or become satisfied with yourself, someone else will see you slacking off and, at that moment, they may try to pass you.

6. Perfect yourself in the field of activity or profession you have chosen. A jack of all trades is seldom well paid. Specialize and intensely *desire* to be the best so that people will respect you for your knowledge and ability. Be the best business man, doctor, lawyer, carpenter, mechanic, gardener, fisherman, nurse, artist or truck driver in the entire area where you live.

7. Success is more pleasant when the work you do is appreciated. And people who consider your efforts are useful to them, will appreciate whatever you do.

Whenever you are lazy, apathetic or negligent, you violate *the Law of Evolution* and you must pay, in some manner, for the violation of that Law. You will find that things you want, do not appear. Your dreams do not come true. Your desires are not met. And you get very little help and cooperation because you have made little effort.

There are thousands of fascinating stories of men and women who have started with a handicap of one kind or another. Yet, in spite of the odds, through the energizing Spirit of Creative Mind, they were able to constantly move forward and become a success.

Their success is recorded proof that no matter where you were born and no matter what your education or environment may have been, nothing can hold you back for long if you have *a strong desire* to move forward and *believe* that you can do better.

Keep your mind open and receptive to opportunities that can help you make further progress. Read good books constantly. Listen, analyze and evaluate all that you see and hear. Never get the feeling that you have learned all that you need to know. The minute you do, you begin to grow old and your lack of desire to learn, and your unwillingness to improve yourself will be reflected in the results you gain from life. Others may pass you by in your job and opportunities to make money will be given to others.

With the above in mind, you can see why you are the one who is responsible for whether you will move forward or stand still.

Whenever you make progress and enjoy the blessings such progress can bring, do not be content. Reach out again for more—not selfishly nor with a greedy desire— but reach out because you want to obey this *Law of Evolution* and you are convinced that "with God's help—all things are possible."

Glenn Miller, who built the most popular dance band of all time, learned to play his trombone in the high school band at Fort Morgan, Colorado.

Herbert Hoover, our 31st President, was born of poor

parents on a small farm in West Branch, Iowa. At eight years of age, he was an orphan and had to depend on help from others. To complete his education, he studied hard and worked his way through Stanford University. His first job after graduation was as a common miner at $2.50 for a ten-hour day. At the age of forty, he was a successful mining consultant and a multi-millionaire. He then gave up his mining career to become one of the world's greatest humanitarians.

Colonel John Glenn, the first American astronaut, was raised in the small town of New Concord, Ohio.

Mark Twain was born on a small farm in Missouri, grew up in the river town of Hannibal, ran away from home and, in spite of a limited education, became one of the world's most prolific and best loved writers.

Conrad Hilton was born and raised in the small mining town of San Antonio, New Mexico. While just a young man, he bought a small hotel in the West Texas town of Cisco. After much hard work and many financial difficulties, he succeeded in operating several small hotels on a paying basis. With constant expansion in mind, Conrad Hilton moved into other states and bought larger hotels. Now he is the largest owner of hotels in the world. A feat he could never have accomplished if he had been satisfied to remain in either San Antonio, New Mexico or Cisco, Texas.

Mickey Mantle, the highest paid player in baseball, was raised in the poverty-stricken mining town of Commerce, Oklahoma.

Eddie Cantor was born of poor Russian immigrants on the lower East Side of New York City. He sang and clowned for pennies on street corners. Through constant effort and searching for opportunities, he rose to the top in vaudeville, musical comedy, motion pictures, radio and television.

In 1914, Carl Wickman, a young miner in Hibbing, Minnesota, owned a seven-passenger Huppmobile which he rigged up to carry ten passengers. He charged 15 cents cash to carry other miners four miles to the Mesabi iron-ore range. A few months later, he took on a partner, Andrew Anderson, a blacksmith. Together, they bought another large car and opened a daily round trip to Duluth—90 miles away. That was how the gigantic Greyhound Bus lines was born.

To change and improve the conditions in your life, you must change and improve your thoughts. There is no other way. If you wait for someone else to do it for you, the change or improvement may never occur. You must be willing to move forward on your own. Then you will be cooperating with this *Law of Evolution*. And the sooner you move forward and make the changes necessary, the sooner your life will improve.

No matter what your age, raise your sights. Never stop learning. Look ahead to the future and fill your mind with expectancy.

As you grow older, you become wiser. You learn what not to do. You find that experience replaces inexperience. Faith and confidence replaces fear. Success replaces failure and abundance replaces poverty. You mature and maturity is one of the most pleasant results of this *Law of Evolution*.

Some people say, "What cannot be cured, must be endured." Christ, however, proved that anyone who has an *intense desire* and *a strong belief* can rise above any condition of limitation or lack. He proved that you need not suffer from any physical handicap nor do without the things you need for very long. He proved there is always a way out of every situation and an answer to every problem.

The Truth is——there is no limit to what you can accomplish because God, *the Secret of Success,* is always with you. When you turn to Him for help and guidance, you may be sure that no one can ever keep you down nor disturb your peace of mind for long.

When your thoughts are based on serving the needs of others and you have a *strong desire* to succeed in whatever activity you undertake, you will succeed in due time because those goals you think about long enough and desire to secure through positive action, will eventually be reached.

While that is true, there are people in many areas of the world who do not know about *the Secret of Success* and they do not understand this *Law of Evolution*. As a result, they continue to live in poverty while there is an abundance of wealth close at hand.

The aborigines of Northern Australia, whom you read about in Chapter One, are a good example of this.

In other areas, there are people who believe in progress and they have a *desire* to get up and grow. They focus their eyes on the abundance and say, "With God's help, I know I can have my share."

Such a man was Walt Disney. He spent his early years on a small farm in Marcelline, Missouri. As he grew older, he found little opportunity at home. Though he never finished high school, he has become fabulously successful.

His vivid imagination and high moral sense have created animated cartoons, nature films, movies and television shows that have enriched the lives of millions of people of all ages all over the world.

His *Disneyland* is one of the most famous cities in the United States. It was started because he found that most amusement parks were "dirty, unpleasant places run by tough-looking people. None of the customers seemed to be having any fun, so I could see there was a need for something new."

The old way was not good enough. Walt Disney created something better. As a reward for his efforts, his *Disneyland* now entertains more than 5,000,000 people each year who are willing to spend more than $45,000,000 to enjoy it.

Good ideals and honest principles are important if you are to be successful in whatever you do. That is why you must carefully choose your friends and find an environment that will allow you to develop and preserve those ideals and principles.

Good friends will always help you to keep your ideals. They will encourage you and help you to move forward.

Bad friends, however, believe too much in mediocrity and comformity. They may try to pull you down or discourage you from doing better. Too often they are jealous of your success. They prefer that you remain on their own level and they may ridicule your desire to improve yourself.

There are many people with such a negative state of mind. That is why there are more followers than leaders. And that is why you will always find plenty of opportunity and room at the top.

Whenever people criticize or resent anyone who does not conform to the mediocre standards under which they live, it is because they do not understand this *Law of Evolution* which requires that every living thing shall improve, move forward, and reach out for something that is just a little better.

Any person, place or thing that "holds you back" or "ties you down" without a reasonable and acceptable explanation, violates this important *Law of Evolution*. Such restrictions are against God's universal plan for perfection and growth and eventual Heaven on earth.

Whenever you live or work in a way that opposes God's plan for perfection, then both you and the one who restrains you must eventually work in cooperation with His plan—according to this *Law of Evolution*—or you must suffer in some way from the consequence that such an attitude and lack of cooperation can bring.

To secure the greatest amount of progress, it is necessary to plan things which can result in a large amount of good for other people. No force that is evil or harmful can succeed for very long because God gives evil no power.

Good which is the Divine Spirit manifesting Itself, will always overcome evil just as surely as the light will overcome the darkness.

That is the reason why slavery had to be abolished. It is the reason why communism, socialism and facism are concepts of government that are fundamentally wrong because they are man-made and contrary to God's will for freedom of expression and growth for all individuals.

It is also the reason why men like Napoleon, Hitler and Al Capone, the boss of Chicago's gangsters, were not able to achieve lasting success.

Whenever you find you cannot live or work in harmony with some other person, whether it be your relative, your marriage partner, a fellow employee or a neighbor, it is easier to secure that harmony if you realize that you cannot criticize or ridicule the efforts of someone else and expect to get cooperation and good results. It is in violation of this *Law of Evolution.*

Wives nag their husbands, but the husband resents it and, oftentimes, gets worse. Employers criticize their employees and the employee, in return, will often do a poorer job.

Such criticism and ridicule leads to resentment and the person criticized will often refuse to listen to what you have to say.

The only way you can correct and improve another person is to make certain you give that person a large amount of praise, respect and love.

The larger the amount you give, the easier it will be to secure his attention. Then you can gain his cooperation and help him to make the correction and improvement you desire.

The reason is—praise, respect and love are positive forces that help people expand. They will always bring you praise, respect and love in return because they enable the soul of human beings to grow in a natural and beneficial way.

They make it easy for men and women to improve themselves because praise, respect and love are the fundamental elements that make *the Law of Evolution* work more easily and effectively.

When individuals do not understand this *Law of Evolution,* they find their life more difficult and unpleasant. That is one of the reasons why domineering fathers and mothers often "lose" their children. It is the reason why overbearing husbands and nagging wives go through life unhappy or else seek relief through a divorce. It is also the reason why some employers, who force their employees to work against their will, eventually lose the better ones and will often receive poor workmanship from those employees who do not leave.

Those who do not understand will contend that we do not need to change, we should not improve. If they live in poverty, they will tend to believe in poverty and, thereby, cause themselves to remain in that unfortunate condition. If they are in an area of unemployment, they will tend to believe in unemployment and refuse to go where jobs are more plentiful or try to find ways to create more jobs. If they are handicapped or held back in any way, they will tend to believe in that handicap or limitation.

Such people will try to prove there is merit in "the old way," "the way we live now and it should not be changed." But arguing against this Law does not prove it to be wrong.

This *Law of Evolution* and the three Laws that follow (Compensation, Prosperity and Non-Resistance) are easy to prove. All you need to do is follow them. Then your path towards success in whatever you do becomes easy.

Whenever millions of people all over the world have a

complete understanding of these four Laws, then peace on earth and harmony among nations will arrive amazingly soon. Business, both nationwide and local, will improve and families will enjoy a greater amount of happiness and contentment.

Because that is true, you should do everything you can to promote a greater understanding and awareness of these Spiritual Laws.

They should be taught in every schoolroom, in every business, in every Sunday School and in every church in the world.

And the more people you help, the more help you will receive in return.

8

The Law of Compensation

EVERYTHING you think about and everything you do is subject to *the Law of Compensation.*

This is the Law based on *the Truth* that "Whatsoever a man soweth, that shall he also reap."*

Under this Law, whatever you give, you will receive. Every thought you express and every condition you create in the lives of others will return to you in the same spirit.

If you wish other people good luck—good luck will eventually come to you. If you wish someone bad luck—bad luck will come to you. If you try to cheat someone—someone will find a way to cheat you.

If you lie to other people—other people will lie to you. If you criticize others—you will, in turn, be criticized. If you resent others—there will be others who will resent you. If you hate someone—someone will hate you. If you love other people—other people will love you.

Your thoughts have the power to bring about whatever you believe. But you must remember to express only good thoughts backed by consideration, respect and love.

If your thoughts are positive, constructive and kindly, you will receive positive results in return and you will enjoy success in many of the things you do.

If, on the other hand, your thoughts are negative, pessimistic or unpleasant, you will experience conditions in your life that can lead to unhappiness, sickness and failure.

---

* Galatians 6:7

The reason is—you cannot sow negative thoughts like, "I don't care," "It can't be done" or "I don't know how" and reap beneficial results.

If your thoughts consist of criticism, hate, jealousy, revenge or greed, such thoughts will eventually come back to you. And you, in turn, will experience criticism, hate, jealousy, revenge or greed. Your life is then filled with disharmony and many forms of tormenting conditions.

But, if your thoughts consist of love, service to others, praise and appreciation, then you will experience a greater amount of harmony, peace of mind and love.

That is true because the world gives back to you exactly what you give out to the world.

Those people who believe in war do not understand *the Secret of Success*. And they have not learned the wisdom of Christ's admonition, "Thy will Father, not my will, be done."

And those people who live in poverty do not understand *the Secret of Success*. Nor have they learned how to serve and fill the needs of others.

As you read in Chapter One, the money you receive is in direct relation to the amount of service you give. So, if you want to earn more money, you must plan and develop ways to serve more people, more efficiently. For the more people you serve, the more money you will receive in return for that service.

If your work or profession helps ten or twenty people, then your income will be small. If it helps one hundred people, your income will be larger. If it helps thousands or even millions as many inventions and services do, then it is possible for you to earn a considerable fortune.

Henry Ford proved that fact. When other companies were making one car per day, Ford said, "People need cars to save time and lighten their work load. Let's build them faster." He then worked out mass production methods that enabled his company to build one new car every minute for several months each year.   And many days, he built as many as four cars a minute.   Such a desire to serve others helped Henry Ford to become America's first billionaire.

Colonel Sanders ran a restaurant in the small mountain town of Corbin, Kentucky and developed an unusual recipe for fried chicken.   He had a *desire* to serve more people and found that, through the medium of franchising, he could serve his special recipe to millions of chicken lovers all over the United States.   His idea spread rapidly and now "Colonel Sanders Kentucky Fried Chicken" is sold in restaurants throughout the United States and in several foreign countries.

When you clearly *understand* this *Law of Compensation* and constantly follow it, your road through life is smoother. Business improves and money will come to you more easily.

Like any important Law, if you obey It, you will live in peace and harmony.   But, if you fail to observe Its wisdom, you will have to suffer the unfortunate reactions that can result.

It is like the paddle-ball you may have played with.   Hit the ball easy and it comes back easy.   Hit it hard and it comes back hard.   Hit it in whatever direction you will—forwards, backwards, sidewards—it will still come back to you with the same amount of force with which you sent it out.

Start walking down the street and the paddle-ball will move along with you.   If the rubber band would not break, you could hit the ball with all your might in an effort to get rid of it; but, even though it traveled a hundred miles and seem too far away to return, it would still come back to you.

That is a very simple illustration of how exacting *the Law of Compensation* affects your life as a result of your thoughts and your actions.

Christ said, "The Kingdom of Heaven is within." And, because the Kingdom of Heaven (the creative spirit of your Super-Conscious Mind) is within, you have all of the power and all of the help you need to change your present conditions and improve the environment in which you now live.

Heaven means peace of mind, health, harmony and freedom from worry and fear. So when you continually think about things that are good, you will eventually experience good things. Good things will come.

Hell, of course, is the opposite of Heaven. Because of wrong thoughts, you can experience sickness, worry, loneliness and a loss of income.

You can experience hell on earth by being resentful, expressing hate or anger, quarreling with your friends and neighbors or causing any other condition that is contrary to this important Law or contrary to any other important Law you read about in this book.

Christ said, "Judge not that ye be not judged. For with what judgment ye judge, ye shall be judged."* This means that if you judge others harshly, you must be ready and willing to be judged harshly in return. If you wish something unpleasant to happen to someone else or if you would like to see them harmed in any way, you must be ready to receive unpleasantness or bear the harm that will surely come into your life.

By knowing *the Truth* and understanding this *Law of Compensation,* you become wiser. You find that you dare not wish anything done to someone else that you are not willing to have done to yourself.

If someone hurts you, let them. They do not know or understand the foolishness of their deed. You, in turn, will find it wise to not retaliate in kind.

If everyone understood this important Law and lived by

---

* Matthew 7:1

it, there would no longer be any injustice or unpleasantness
left in this world.

Think a moment. Have you had some good luck lately?
You may be certain that you deserved it. Sometime in
the past few days or months, you set in motion the Law that
guarantees to return to you the good that you now receive.
You spoke well of someone, you helped someone or you
gave someone words of encouragement. No matter what
you said or did, the very moment you expressed love,
encouragement or service to anyone or to any group, you set
in motion *the Law of Compensation* that would eventually
return to you the same amount of good.

It is not "luck" you received, it is compensation—the
compensation you deserve.

Now let us assume that you have been having a bit of "bad
luck." If you are perfectly honest with yourself and analyze
every word you spoke and every act you committed in the
past few weeks, you will find that you have spoken words of
criticism or hate, you were angry with someone, you tried to
take something away from someone, or you tried to get
something for nothing. Isn't that true? Of course it is.

Did you forget to help someone when they needed help?
Did you ignore someone when they needed encouragement?
Did you put over a "fast deal" so that you gained while someone else lost? Did you wish someone bad luck? Did you
take something without giving some money or service in return? You say—you did. Then you will soon experience
the effects of this *Law of Compensation.*

You cannot escape it. Like the paddle-ball, no matter
which way you move, no matter how hard you try to forget
it, the results of your unfortunate actions will always come
back to you.

The important thing is to stop doing those things. Fortunately, you can minimize the wrong thoughts you may
have expressed by immediately, and from now on, thinking

only of good thoughts and wishing the best for those same persons, places or things.

Your life will be more happy and successful if you will find ways to do good instead of expecting it. The reason is—"Bread cast upon the waters" still "comes back double."

Have you ever seen a person who hoarded money, living happily? Have you ever seen a person who paid his bills in a grudging manner, living happily? Have you ever seen a person who lived primarily for himself, living happily? No. The reason is, such a person violates *the Law of Compensation.* His thoughts and actions are centered around getting and keeping what he has due to the fear it might be lost.

Giving, on the other hand, like love, creates an atmosphere that leads to expansion and it opens the door so that you can receive a larger amount of good and have it more abundantly.

Success comes from *believing* in the thoughts that will bring success. You cannot "sow" wrong thoughts and "reap" right experiences. You cannot believe in evil and receive good. You cannot hurt someone and expect that you will remain untouched.

Since that is true, you must continually guide your thoughts so they will bring about the type of conditions you sincerely *desire.*

Give a large measure of respect and love and you will, in return, receive a large measure of respect and love. Sow thoughts of good will, peace, prosperity and happiness and you will reap large measures of the same.

When your thoughts are guided by an honest desire to serve others and you express thoughts that are constructive and agreeable, the reaction you receive will also be constructive and agreeable.

You will then experience harmony and greater success because your thoughts are guided in that direction.

Thoughts you express that aim to harm someone or de-

prive someone of what they own will result in some form
of punishment or unhappiness. The reason is—all things
which are evil are contrary to God's plan for perfection.
Their nature is destructive. That is why evil thoughts and
actions will eventually destroy themselves.

For example, if you steal, you must go to jail. If you
attack someone, you may be killed by that same person or
someone else close by. If you deceive someone or deprive
someone of their rights, you may lose many friends and find
yourself without the backing you need.

You can see that, once you understand and follow *the
Law of Compensation,* it is easy to have "good luck."

Say nice things to the same people you have been criticiz-
ing. Express love and respect for the same people with
whom you have been angry. Do something *for* people—
instead of expecting so much *from* people.

Believe in all of the good things that exist—then watch
your life improve.

Christ said, "Love thy neighbor as thyself" and "Do unto
others as you would have others do unto you." Those two
sentences contain the answer to how to be happy and get
along more easily with everyone you meet.

You have heard those thoughts expressed by other people
for many years. And it is possible you may have said, "I
love everybody—except" and then you name one or two
others who irritate you. But, of course, if there is some one
person you do not love, then, obviously you do not love
everyone.

In order to gain the utmost cooperation from others in
your desire for success, you must do all that you can to
benefit other people. You must bring the light of knowledge and the peace of understanding to those who do not
have them.

All of the good you receive is given to you because you
offered something good to someone else either now or at

some time in the past. And, anything bad that you receive, comes to you because some time in the past, you wished someone bad luck, you failed to help someone when help was needed, or you did something that hurt someone else.

The Law of Compensation requires that, if you pray to God to help you overcome sickness, worry or a financial problem and your prayer is answered, you must show your gratitude; *first*, by thanking God for His help and, *second*, by immediately passing along to someone else or to some deserving group a portion of the blessing you have received.

If you received money, part of that money should immediately be set aside or given to someone else. If you receive relief from worry or regained your health, you should immediately try to make someone else happy or help them, in some way, to feel better.

Analyze your innermost thoughts, study your actions and see whether or not you are carefully observing this important Law in your life every day.

When you give, you must give willingly and unselfishly without any thought of return. If you do, you will be blessed. If you fail to observe this Law, then you will not be entitled to receive additional help in the future.

In brief, *the Law of Compensation* can be summed up in these words:

If you want to get more—you must first give more. (You have to give a push to the paddle-ball before you can expect it to come back to you.)

If you want to get more out of the world—you must first put more into the world.

If you want to earn more—you must first learn more.

9

The Law of Prosperity

MANY of the problems bothering people today are financial ones. Yet financial problems can easily be overcome—if you understand and follow *the Law of Prosperity*.

The Truth is—wealth, not poverty, is the way of life God has in mind for you. He wants you to live richly and well because it proves to everyone you meet that His love is always available to all those who will turn to Him as an ever-loving Father and accept the good things He has to offer.

Think for a moment and you will realize that there is plenty of everything for all those who want to make an effort to serve others and earn their share.

There is plenty of money, plenty of jobs, plenty of homes, plenty of cars and plenty of opportunities for creating more.

It is necessary, therefore, to see this world of plenty in its proper light and realize that all of the things that exist around you are the result of the creative spirit of Infinite Mind.

There is certainly more today than twenty years ago. And there is many times more now than one hundred or two hundred years ago.

Since it is the nature of God to continually provide more of everything whenever they are desired and necessary, you may be certain that tomorrow there will be more jobs more money and more opportunities than exist today. And, in the years to come, so long as God's will is obeyed, there will be even more.

The reason is—progress and plenty are a part of God's plan. But he requires that everything He has made shall have harmony and balance. Whenever harmony and balance are lacking, disorder and confusion result and prosperity is then more difficult to obtain.

The Law of Prosperity is as necessary to maintain this harmony and balance as *the Law of Gravity*. It will work effectively in your favor so long as your attitude of mind is based on the fundamental *Truth*—

> "Give and it shall be given unto you; good
> measure, pressed down, shaken together and
> running over."*

If you continually *believe* and *practice* that *Truth,* you will never worry about the supply of any material thing you need—money, clothes, food, a job, a home, etc. In due time, they will come to you somehow from somewhere.

That fact is true because God, the Infinite Source of all good, will never let you down.

Whatever you need, He already knows about that need. He wants you to have plenty of everything and a supply will always be furnished or made available to meet that need—provided you follow *the Law of Prosperity.*

The only time you will lack whatever material things you need or be without money is when you stop believing there is plenty of everything available and you allow yourself to believe that "times are tough," "money is scarce," where is the money coming from" or "I can't afford to give."

Such negative thoughts and attitudes are self-defeating.

---

* Luke 6:38

They turn your mind away from God and make it difficult for you to see His infinite supply.

If your parents or friends have spoken these negative words, then you have been led to believe that poverty, limitation and lack of opportunity are a normal part of your life.

As a result of hearing and believing such thoughts, you have become accustomed to negative habits which must be corrected.

New ideas and beliefs must be formed. You need to direct your thoughts more often to God and allow His Super-Conscious Mind to help you. Then ways will be opened up and you will find that money and opportunities of every kind will flow more easily and naturally to you.

The Truth is—no circumstances and no person can hold you down or keep you from securing whatever you want unless you, yourself, allow it to happen.

When you talk with people who are short of money, many of them will tell you they do not aspire to great things. They want little out of life. And they try to convince others that their lack of worldly goods is a condition that cannot be helped.

That is not true. Instead, they are satisfied with the way they live. They lack *the desire* to do better and they are seldom interested in finding ways to rise above their present situation.

They do not realize that *"Whatsoever a man believes that shall he also receive."*

Because millions of people do not *understand* that statement, they live in conditions of poverty while all around them is a world full of opportunity and abundance.

Robert G. LeTourneau, at the age of 30, was unemployed, had a family to support and was $5,000 in debt. But, in 1919, he discovered *the Secret of Success.* He overcame his impoverished situation, invented many new machines, eventually employed thousands of men and earned many millions of dollars.

Mr. LeTourneau stated his views on money in this way, "I put my own confidence in God. I don't know what the future holds, but I do know Who holds the future. If He wants you to make money to serve His purposes, you'll make it. If He doesn't want you to have money, He'll find ways to take it from you, no matter how much you might have."

Surveys have been taken of people who live in poverty-stricken areas to find out what could be done to help them. Several hundred people were asked this question, "If you had more money, would that solve your problem?"

The answer many gave was "No."

Their main problem was not lack of money. If they had more money, they would spend it on liquor, cigarettes, entertainment, travel and many other temporary pleasures which would not, in any way, improve their financial condition.

They had no *desire* to buy or own things of permanent value. Therefore, as soon as they spent the extra money, they would be poor again.

The above survey proves that money alone will not cure poverty. The cure lies in helping such people realize that an increased amount of money is always possible—from a more dependable Source.

They need to be taught *the Truth* that there is a great Creative Force within them called God that will always help them to increase their supply—if they will increase their *desire* and obey *the Laws of Evolution, Compensation and Prosperity.*

They must learn to sow before they can reap. They must learn to give service before they can get. And they must find ways to increase their knowledge so they can have more faith in their ability to produce.

This will enable them to broaden their horizons so they

can focus more of their attention on progress instead of allowing their thoughts to dwell on failure.

When people look for continued aid or a "hand out," they are ignoring this important *Law of Prosperity*. Their minds are directed towards getting, instead of giving or sowing first.

They try to get something for nothing. But such an attitude is against God's Law and cannot, in any way, lead to success.

They must learn how to evolve, move forward and seek a better way of life according to God's Laws or suffer the consequences—which, in many cases, is a life of unhappiness, limitation and lack.

By stimulating their *desire* to do something rather than nothing and working with this Creative Force, ideas will come that can help them to solve their problems and enable them to rise above the conditions under which they live.

As a result of raising their sights, they will be able to secure a greater amount of the good things that God is so willing to give to those who love Him and look to Him for help.

"But," you may say, "when people have so little, what can they give?"

They can always give something. Talent, time and love cost nothing. They are things everyone can give regardless of age, income and circumstances.

And the more willingly such people give, the more good things they will receive in return. So long as the gift is made, God will supply them with some form of good as compensation.

Furthermore, those who want to earn more money, must develop a sincere and continuous *desire* to serve others. For the greater the desire and effort to serve, the greater the amount of help and money they will receive in return.

Some people, however, say, "Money is evil." But money is not evil. Money is good. It is "the love of money" that "is evil."

Money is a convenient medium of exchange. It can do a great deal of good. And the more money you have, the more good you can do.

"Like an arm or a leg," Henry Ford said, "you must either use money or lose it."

Having the money you need or not having it, depends a great deal on your attitude towards it. The more faith you express in the available supply of God, the more money you will eventually receive. And the less faith you express, the less money you will receive.

When you are afraid to take a chance for fear of losing the money you have, it tends to make more money difficult to obtain.

The importance of right thinking in an effort to create prosperity, is illustrated in the parable of the three men who were given the talents (an old Jewish coin).

One man was given five talents. He immediately put them to work and earned five more.

By doing this, he proved *the Law of Evolution*—arise, act, move forward and grow; *the Law of Compensation*— give before you receive; and *the Law of Prosperity*—believe in the things that bring success and success will come.

Another man received two talents. He also put them to work and earned two more.

The third man was given one talent. He was afraid of losing it so, in order to make certain he would have that talent when his master returned, he buried it.

By such an action, he broke the three *Laws of Evolution, Compensation and Prosperity.*

When the master returned, each man was asked to account for each of the talents he had been given.

The first man said, "Lord, thou deliverest unto me five talents; behold, I have gained besides them five talents more." And the second man said, "Lord, thou deliverest unto me two talents; behold I have gained two other talents besides them."

The Lord said unto both of them, "Well done, thou good and faithful servant; thou hast been faithful over a few things I will make thee ruler over many things; enter into the joy of the Lord."*

Then he turned to the third man who said, "Lord, I was afraid and hid thy talent in the earth."

The Lord rebuked him saying, "Thou wicked and slothful servant, thou oughtest to have put my money to the exchangers and then, at my coming, I should have received mine own with usary. Take, therefore, your talent and give unto him which hath ten talents. For unto everyone that hath (followed the three Laws of Evolution, Compensation and Prosperity) more shall be given, and he shall have abundance; but from him that hath not (followed the three Laws) even that which he hath, shall be taken away."

The above parable illustrates that money, like seeds in the hands of a farmer, should be used and not put upon a shelf or placed where that money cannot grow.

Giving, like love, always opens the way for receiving. It is just as essential, therefore, to give as to get. And, when you obey this *Law of Prosperity,* your supply will always increase.

If you are afraid of being poor and hold onto every cent, you will attract the very things you fear.

You will lose the great amount of good that can come to you when your money is put to work effectively in the right places. And you will experience poverty or unhappiness of one sort or another.

* Matthew 25:14–30

While that is true, poverty of money is only one of the results of a limited, poverty-type thinking.

There is also the poverty of ideas which results when you believe you have a limited amount of funds. And, of course, when you are short of ideas, you will also be short of money.

Your supply of ideas will increase as soon as you share your ideas with others. They, in turn, will give you ideas and you will then have more ideas than just your own.

There may be times when you can see no solution to your problems. And it may be difficult to have enough *faith*.

If you will be positive, however, and continue to *believe,* your faith will increase and the money, ideas and solutions you need will come to you more easily.

If you desire wealth, you must first fell that wealth is possible. Whenever you "see" money coming to you, know it is coming to you and *believe* you will get it, you will certainly receive it in some form.

You must hold that picture clearly and firmly in your mind. You must never doubt for a second and you must never worry. Expect increased prosperity and increased prosperity will come to you. If you lessen your belief, then, as a consequence, you will lessen the amount you receive.

"Commit thy way unto the Lord; trust also in him; and He shall bring it to pass."*

You must realize that everything in the entire world belongs to God. We are simply stewards for Him. Therefore, it is easy to understand why it is so necessary to treat God fairly and with a grateful heart.

Imagine how long you could keep a business partner happy if you failed to thank him for his help and then, on pay-day, handed him a few dollars.

"But," you may say, "It is necessary to pay human beings

* Psalms 37:5

for their help." That is true, but it is even more important to pay God for His help.

The reason is—God is the source of all your substance and it is wise to recognize His ownership.

God made it possible for you to have the strength, the ability and the desire to earn the money you receive. He also supplies you with the air, sunshine, water, minerals, trees, flowers, plants and everything you need. Then He wisely makes certain that all of those good things cooperate with you so that you can always be certain of using them as they were intended to be used—to help other people enjoy life more abundantly.

All He asks is that you be grateful to Him and appreciate the use of the many wonderful things He has loaned to you. And *loaned* it is, because you cannot take anything with you when you finally leave this earth.

The story is told of the farmer who swept his hand over the broad acres of his farm and said, "Bishop, this morning you said the land I own was not all mine. Don't I own all of this?"

The Bishop replied with a smile, "My friend, ask me again one hundred years from now."

In the final analysis, you see, you actually own nothing in this world. Everything has been *loaned* to you by God. It is His desire that you be a good steward and properly use all of the things He has made available.

He wants you to take care of them, develop them and leave them better than when you found them.

Tithing (giving one-tenth of one's income) is one of the ways millions of people use when they want to say, "Thank you," to God. As a result of their unselfishness and their willingness to be grateful, they are often rewarded with an increase.

"But," you may say, "If I give away one-tenth of my income, I will only have nine-tenths left to spend."

The Truth is—when you live by the spiritual *Law of Prosperity*, you are willing to make God a partner in your life. You add His power and intelligence to your own ability and you are able to accomplish much more than you would normally accomplish without His help.

If, on the other hand, you do not give one-tenth of your income or do not give of your time in an effort to help others, then you are seriously violating this *Law of Prosperity* and God will eventually take that 10% away from you in some other way. You will lose it through sickness, accident, unemployment, theft or a business loss.

By recognizing God as your partner and paying the 10% to which He is entitled, you actually gain instead of lose. You get an extra 100% worth of help for only 10%.

God, you see, is not selfish. He is willing to help you for a very small amount. The result is, with God helping you, you are worth 200% instead of just 90%.

The right viewpoint, you see, is important.

Many of the most successful men in the world have been consistent tithers.

Robert G. LeTourneau has become rich both financially and in peace of mind by actually reversing the process. He set up the R. G. LeTourneau Foundation and arranged for 90% of his profits to go for the development of God's work while he takes only 10%. The reason is, Mr. Le-Tourneau credits all of his ability, his ideas and his multi-million dollar fortune to God's help and, he reasons, "I believe" he said, "since God has done most of the work, He should get most of the pay."

Such an attitude is unusual but, to Mr. LeTourneau, it makes sense. It does have merit and the profits of his gigantic machinery company grow larger every year.

Another business man I know was very successful when tithing only 10%. One day he said to me, "I believe I will start giving 20%. His business grew and prospered.

A few years later, I asked him what he thought of his plan for giving 20%. He replied with a smile, "I can only prove its wisdom by showing you my income tax statement for last year." It showed he had paid a tax on net earnings of $51,000.00.

He was satisfied that God had proven to be a very good partner.

Systematic giving to promote whatever purposes are helpful to God, is one of the most effective ways to prove how *the Law of Prosperity* can work in your favor.

The attitude of "getting," "holding" and lack of sharing, interferes with the free flow of supply. Just as surely as holding down the brakes of your automobile slows down its progress and closing a faucet shuts off your supply of water.

The business or professional man whose main interest is to get all he can with very little thought to giving will eventually find his business falling off.

The farmer who works his land (which we know is really God's land) without returning some material benefit to the soil, will soon exhaust the fertility of that land and his crops will either be meager or stunted.

The employee, who works for wages and fails to be grateful to God for supplying him with the opportunity to work and prosper, will also fail. Or he will experience the result of his lack of gratitude by having a sickness, an accident or some other form of loss.

Much "getting," you see, and very little "giving" can often lead to poverty, illness or a decrease in supply.

When you give freely with a willing heart, you actually increase your ability because *the Secret of Success* will help you secure a greater amount of prosperity.

People will give to you because you are willing to give to them. And, if people are so willing to give to you, then, obviously, you have increased your potential by giving.

Henry Ford knew this secret of prosperity in a time when other business men of his day believed in small wages. They believed that greater profits are earned by keeping wages low. But Ford had the proper attitude.

When wages were $1 per day, he said, "We will pay our men $5 per day. Then they will be able to buy more cars."

Business men everywhere spoke out against such a large raise. They believed that Ford's policy would eventually bankrupt them. Workers rushed to the Ford plant by the thousands. Bankers urged him to "stop such foolishness and run your business in a business-like manner."

Ford's answer was, "Go and do the same. Your business will soon be better." And their business *was* better. Later he raised the daily wage again to $7 per day and the American standard of living was improved some more.

By such willingness to give, Ford was rewarded with additional orders and his company became the first to produce more than a million cars a year.

The McCormick Tea and Spice Company of Baltimore, Maryland is another organization that has proved the wisdom of "giving" in business.

They decided to give every executive, every employee in their plant, every salesman and every truck driver the opportunity to express himself. They called this new plan of cooperation "Multiple Management." Special committees were set up to discuss and decide on answers to questions of policy, sales and production.

Each committee went over all of the ideas that were submitted and the best ideas were passed on to each department head to be carried out. Every employee had a chance to "tell the boss" how to run the business. As a result of this spirit of giving, the company gained by receiving hundreds of good ideas from employees who enjoyed the closer relationship with the company.

That same policy is used in a smaller way by many other companies in the form of a "suggestion box."

But a greater amount of cooperation might be gained by those same companies if they were to adopt the entire "Multiple Management" plan.

By giving their key employees more opportunity to participate in the operation of the company, they are likely to receive more from their employees in return.

So you see that, by adopting a sincere and consistent attitude of giving, you do not lose—you can actually gain.

To be a financial success, you must identify yourself with financial success. Feel rich and successful no matter how much money you have. Wear good clothes and drive a nice car. By *feeling* financially secure, you *prove* you have *faith* and you will soon receive money, a check, a gift, or an offering of a new job.

Such benefits may come from unusual sources. They will come if you *believe* because *the Law of Prosperity* never fails. *Only you can fail by failing to believe.*

The story is told of a group of nuns in an orphanage in France. They had planned a picnic for the children and found they were short of enough food to go around. They counted their money and discovered their small amount of change would buy only a little additional food.

They were on the verge of calling off the picnic when the Monsignor of the parish arrived. He found out about their difficulty, asked the nuns for the coins, then went out in the yard and threw them as far as he could.

The nuns were shocked, but he explained his action with these words, "You have placed your faith in the wrong place. God will provide."

Within the hour, a group of women from the village arrived with baskets of food to provide more than enough for the picnic. They had come because they had a desire to provide a picnic for the orphans and they gathered together the supplies.

Hoarding, like waste, is a sin because hoarding helps no one. And, if it helps no one, then it is contrary to the three Divine Laws of *Evolution, Compensation* and *Prosperity*.

The more of God's laws you break, the more unhappiness you will eventually suffer as a consequence.

Too many people believe they must "save for a rainy day." But rain may never come and such a habit is a violation of this very important *Law of Prosperity*. It is in giving and in spending—provided it is done wisely—that you cooperate with this Law and make it work for you.

In return for obeying this *Law of Prosperity* and proving your *faith,* then God, as a reward or compensation, will give you more.

You, alone, can increase your supply of money and ideas because you, alone, are the one who needs to be positive. God, *the Secret of Success,* is always positive.

As His partner, you will get along with Him better if you agree with His wisdom—instead of arguing against it.

"But" you may say, "I must be realistic. When I have only a small amount of money or cannot see where more is coming from, I must be careful and hold on to what I have."

Such thinking is negative. It is not realistic because it displays weakness—not strength. It shows a lack of *faith.* It is a result of *the false belief* so many of us have been taught.

So long as you limit your thoughts and limit your belief, you will be unable to receive all of the benefits this *Law of Prosperity* has to offer. Such an attitude creates conditions that limit the amount of money or other supply you can eventually receive.

When you fully understand *the Law of Prosperity,* it will

work in your favor. If you are positive, if you have enough *faith and believe,* and you can "see" yourself receiving the things you need, then you may be certain that, at the proper time, you will receive them.

God does not limit you. You only limit yourself. You can only climb a ladder by looking up—not down nor sideways.

If you are working for a salary, do not allow yourself to stay in a rut. If you do, you may be unhappy with the result. Say to yourself, "I am going to do better. I am going to study and learn so I can earn more."

If your present job, for some reason, limits your opportunity and you know you can, in some way, serve more people, either get another job where the opportunity is greater or, take a part-time job and earn some money on the side.

Your part-time job can often be developed into a full-time job that will offer you more chance for growth and income. If you are working on a commission, set your sales quota higher and higher. Then *believe* you will reach it. There is no other way to move ahead on a sound and honest basis.

When you *believe* in success, happiness and abundance, and have a *desire* for those good things, your *belief* and your *desire* will draw those things to you. In fact, you will receive those benefits in exact proportion to your *desire* and your *belief.*

So, to make your progress more certain, spend much of your time developing your *desire.* Then increase your *belief* and you will automatically increase the amount you will receive.

The little colored boy with the shoe-shine box who says, "Shine, Mister, only 10¢ per shoe," has the *desire* to shine shoes and the *belief* you will accept. Even though you might say "no," he knows that if he maintains that *desire* and *belief,* the law of averages will always assure him of a certain number of shoes to shine.

The little six-year-old who says, "Daddy, I need a nickel," has the desire and belief you will give it to him. The employee, who has carefully learned his job and prepared himself, exhibits his *desire* and *belief* when he walks in to see the boss and says, "I am ready to take on more responsibility and I want a promotion and a raise."

If the promotion is available and the boss can recognize the desire to do better, then the employee with that amount of ambition will get the new opportunity.

Many people, unfortunately, believe in the wrong things. They believe opportunities no longer exist. They believe that money is scarce. They believe that others can do a job better. And they believe they might fail if they try.

In spite of the fact there is plenty of everything, their negative thoughts and lack of *belief* keeps them living in conditions that prevent them from realizing their true God-given potential.

The Truth is—having an abundance of wealth is the natural way of life because it is the result of the creative spirit of God expressing Himself.

Poverty, on the other hand, is unnatural because it is contrary to what God wants you to have. And it is the consequence that results from failing to obey *the Law of Compensation* and a lack of *belief* in the *Law of Prosperity*.

You must always be *aware* of the plenty that is close at hand. Then you will receive more of the good things that God can always create and supply to everyone of us.

In his book, "Acres of Diamonds," Russell Conwell tells the story of a man who had a great desire to be rich. He knew that, if he could ever get away from his farm and go to where plenty of money was available, he would have his share. He sold his farm and the new tenant, who was not so eager to become rich, found acres of diamonds on the farm and became fabulously wealthy.

While the book goes on to illustrate many important

points concerning prosperity, the moral of the story is—there are many opportunities close to home.

Look there first.

Never set a limit upon what you can do or upon what you can earn. The limit you set will cause the creative spirit of the *Law of Prosperity* to slow down and It will work less effectively in your favor.

It is like keeping the lights in your room turned down low so you can save electricity. The little you save in electricity will be more than eaten up by the extra amount you will have to spend overcoming the strain on your eyes. Or, to put it another way, it is like driving down the road in your car with your brakes on.

This *Law of Prosperity,* like each of the other Laws of the Universal Mind, works in direct proportion to your use of it. Use it often and your chances of success are improved. Fail to use it and financial problems, unhappiness and restrictions of many kinds will arise.

Opportunities will also be lost because opportunities come only to those who, like the first two men in the parable of the talents, are willing to invest their time, attention and money and thereby receive a higher rate of return.

Temporary saving is good provided it is meant for an immediate goal. On the other hand, saving is imprudent when it is done because you are afraid to spend the money you have for fear that more money will not come or more money is not readily available.

I know a woman who carefully saved every possible penny she could, gave the church 50¢ every Sunday, bought the cheapest clothes for her children and managed to save up a few thousand dollars.

But, she had forgotten to follow *the Law of Prosperity.* She did not *believe.* She had also failed to consider God as her partner. Instead of the 10% which was His rightful share, she believed the 50¢ donation to the church would satisfy Him. And I have known her to refuse to help anyone who came to her door "Because," she said, "I cannot afford to take care of other people."

Her every action and every thought displayed a lack of knowledge of this *Law of Prosperity*. One day, her son had a serious accident. During the several months he spent in the hospital, her savings dwindled until only a few dollars were left. She had violated *the Law of Prosperity* and, as a consequence, she had to learn her lesson the hard way. She lost the 10% she had tried so hard to save.

You may say, "It is a good thing she saved the money or she would not have been able to pay the bills."

No, *the Truth is,* her misfortune came about because her reasoning was based, primarily, on fear. She forgot to follow this important *Law of Prosperity*. As a result, she had to pay one way or another.

She acted as foolishly as the man who had hidden his talent in the earth.

The loss occurred because, as Christ pointed out, "To him that hath not (followed *the Laws of Evolution, Compensation and Prosperity*) even that which he hath, shall be taken away."

Your next question may be, "Then you believe that no one should save money for accidents, sickness, etc." That is exactly right. No one should save for accidents and sickness unless they *believe* in them. When you *believe* in sickness and accidents, then you should save for them for they will surely come, in one form or another. "As ye believe," you see, "It shall be done unto you."

But, if you can honestly and fearlessly *believe* in the Divine Mind and *believe* that sickness and accidents will not come into your life, then like the two men who used their talents so successfully, God will "Make you ruler over many things."

Once you gain complete faith in *the Secret of Success*

you will never need to worry about the future. If sickness or an accident should occur, you will then have the dependable spiritual qualities necessary to succeed and you will find the ways and means to overcome such a situation.

Hundreds of illustrations can be written about people who have *believed* in this *Law of Prosperity* and have seen their fortunes increase. But, to write about so many, would require several volumes.

I can only ask you to *believe* the words of Jesus Christ who said, "Behold the fowls of the air; they sow not, neither do they reap, yet your heavenly Father feedeth them. *Are ye not better than they.* Shall He not much more clothe you, Oh, ye of little faith?"*

A door of opportunity will always open for you. If you should lose a foothold, another will always be provided if you will continue to look and try. A way to succeed will be suggested to you—if you have the *desire* to succeed, have enough *faith* and sincerely believe that success will come.

The man you see begging on the street is actually demonstrating his *belief* in lack and a *desire* to get something for nothing.

That same man, by changing his thoughts can also demonstrate a *belief* in abundance. By *believing*—he can get a job, and having *a strong desire* to get a job—he will get a job and earn more money because he is willing to serve other people rather than wait for other people to serve him.

The more you understand this *Law of Prosperity,* the more good fortune will come to you.

Read this chapter at least once each day for thirty days. Try to follow this *Law* then watch your prosperity increase.

* Matthew 6:26.

Put the three Laws of Evolution, Compensation and Prosperity to work in your own behalf. Try them. You will find they work.

Give a copy of "The Secret of Success" to each and every person you can—for Christmas, a birthday or graduation. Send a copy to your friends, to the high school and college library, to newlyweds and disabled persons.

Make certain it is in every hospital room and in every public library.

Give this book to your employees, social workers and those who work for the government.

It is the perfect gift for newly-married couples who *desire* greater satisfaction from their marriage.

And it should be placed in the hands of every man and woman who must spend some time in a prison.

Let everyone in the world know *"The Secret of Success"* and your own success will also increase.

The more books you place in the hands of others, the more good you will do. And the more good things, as compensation, will be given to you in return.

10

The Law of Non-Resistance

THERE is an old saying that, "Those who live by the sword, shall die by the sword." This means that those who seek trouble always find it. They can blame no one but themselves if their lives are upset or destroyed by wrong thoughts or wrong actions.

Such people would rather fight than reason. They would rather take than give. They would rather hinder than help.

Because their thoughts and actions create friction, they find life difficult rather than easy. The reason is—they do not understand the spiritual *Law of Non-Resistance* so they live in a way that is contrary to *the Secret of Success.*

They do not realize that resistance can be overcome by a persistant expression of love. And disagreements can be overcome by the words, "There must be a better way. Let's find it together."

The Law of Non-Resistance is pointed out many times in the Bible. A few quotations are, "Agree with thine adversary quickly," "Stand still and see the salvation of the Lord (Law)," "Bless your enemies and do good unto them that hurt you," "If a man strikes you on one side of the cheek, turn also the other." "Blessed are the meek (those who are humble and believe in God) for they shall inherit the earth."

You may say, "I don't want to be a door-mat. I am not going to let people push me around."

But *the Truth is*—if you understand *the Law of Non-Resistance* and use it with wisdom, then no one will want to take advantage of you.

In fact, if anyone should take advantage of you, your spirit of non-resistance will, eventually, pay off because you have willingly followed this Law. And God, in some way, will always repay you for your continued sincerity and obedience.

The Bible says, "The way of the transgressor is hard" but "Love conquereth all things."

For nearly two hundred years, the British ruled India. They had complete control of that huge country but India wanted freedom and independence. An armed revolution might have failed and several hundred thousand people might have been killed. Yet Mahatma Gandhi was able to secure that freedom for four hundred million Indians by a continuous program of passive, non-resistance.

It was the first time in the history of the world that such a large nation had secured their independence without firing a shot.

Evil deeds and evil thoughts will eventually destroy themselves because it is contrary to the Laws you have read about in this book. That is why "crime does not pay." Many criminals, however, have become very successful citizens after "serving their time" because they found it was wiser to cooperate with the Laws of Universal Mind rather than fight against them.

Solomon wrote, "It is an honour for a man to cease from strife; for every fool will be meddling."*

Napoleon was one of the world's most successful generals. He prided himself on the fact no one ever pushed him around. But Napoleon finally found it did not pay.

The Duke of Wellington defeated him at the battle of

---

* Proverbs 20:3

Waterloo and he lost the permanent glory he thought such force could create.

When Napoleon was exiled to the island of St. Helena, his active mind began to reason why. Why should a man who had enjoyed so much power and influence be forced to live out his life in disgrace?

In his diary, Napoleon wrote, "Alexander, Caesar, Charlemagne and I founded great empires. But upon what did the creation of our genius depend? Upon force. Jesus Christ alone founded His empire upon love—and, to this very day, millions would die for him."

Napoleon learned too late that, if you resist a situation, you will always have it to contend with. If you fuss or fight with someone, they will fuss or fight with you.

The tree that does not resist the wind will bend with it, but the tree that resists the wind and refuses to bend, may be broken in two.

The answer then is simple. Whenever a situation arises that causes friction, a fuss or a fight, you will find it wise to do as the tree, "Agree with thine adversary" and bend a little.

That is a brief explanation of the meaning behind *the Law of Non-Resistance*. And it is a vital part of *the Secret of Success*.

When a rock is placed over a bush, it will try to grow around that rock. And you can be as wise as that bush. As a human being, you can grow around your circumstance. Through non-resistance, you can create more harmony, increase the number of your friends and eliminate the friction that may cause you trouble.

When you are confronted with a problem or a serious situation, there is only one way to handle it. Don't fight it. Relax and let go. Immediately find a quiet place away from other people and "tune in" the Infinite Mind.

If you strain or try to force a situation, if you criticize or insist that *your* way is the only way, you make that situation more difficult and it will take longer to solve the problem.

The more relaxed you are, the easier it is to receive an answer. It is wise, therefore, to "Stand still, be quiet, and see the salvation of the Lord."

There may be times when other people will say things that irritate you but nothing is ever gained by spite or anger or name-calling. "A soft answer" will always "turn away wrath" and "silence is often golden."

The wisest course, therefore, is *Non-Resistance.*

Christ stated *the Law of Non-Resistance* with these words, "Love thy neighbor as thyself" and "Forgive them that do trespass against you."

He also said, "Resist not evil." He knew that when you resist evil—it will remain and grow. If you keep evil or hate or dislike in your mind, you give them substance and they appear real. If you ignore them, they will fade away or die from lack of attention.

When you lose your temper, you lose control of yourself. You may say or do something you will regret for the rest of your life. And you can lose your friends, upset people where you work or ruin your marriage. All because you became angry over little things that time will prove were not as important as you first believed them to be.

"Let every man be slow to speak and slow to wrath. For the wrath of man worketh not the righteousness of God."*

If you exercise self-control and learn to ignore the small irritations you encounter each day, you will be richly rewarded.

Love, humility, sympathy and understanding are the four great attitudes that can make your life more pleasant and successful. They are the essence of this *Law of Non-Resistance.*

---

* James 1:19

Solomon said, "He that is slow of wrath, is of great understanding." When people become irritated or upset with someone else, you may be certain it is because they do not understand. They criticize that person or judge him without, first, taking the time to *know* why that person thinks or acts the way he does.

I remember a boy in North Carolina who loved to fight and it seemed he had a fight with some other boy every day.

But, one of the boys he always taunted, would always say, "No" and walk away. After being ignored for several weeks, he finally said to this boy, "Come on and fight me. Why don't you fight me?"

"Because I *love* you," the boy replied.

The fighting spirit left him because he could find no logical reason for insisting a fight begin. Later, these two boys became close and devoted friends and remain so to this day.

Will Rogers said, "I've never met a man I didn't like." With that statement, he made life easier and more pleasant for himself. Why? Because he did not require that everyone he met be perfect. He understood them all and accepted them for what they were—good, normal human beings all trying to get along in their own individual way.

He knew that God, in His wisdom, does not create conformity in nature or in human beings. So he accepted people as they were and ignored their human frailties. As a result, he found everyone he met interesting and he loved them for it.

It is easy to be critical and Will Rogers knew that also. But he believed that criticism is a costly way to live. It causes you to lose friends and others will want to stay away from you till you "cool down."

You can also lose the love and affection you seek because criticism, nagging and fault-finding cause the other person to find some way to protect himself. He will shut his mind against you or he may get up and leave your presence.

Others who may not know how to be patient, may voice their own opinion and criticize you in return. Such a violent reaction on their part makes friendship and understanding more difficult.

But there is a way that you can prevent unpleasant arguments and further discussion. Whenever people criticize you, answer them with "Yes, I believe you are right and I am trying my best to correct it."

No one is 100% wrong—so they must be a little bit right. Agree with the point you feel is right, then present your own side of the case.

If friction continues, then relieve the friction as a good mechanic would do. Add more oil in the form of agreement to remove the friction, or stop grinding until you find more ways in which you can agree.

If you want to smooth your way to success, you must make every effort to understand other people and learn the art of forgiveness.

Augusta Rundel wrote a very clear illustration of understanding and forgiveness and it deserves careful consideration.

"When your neighbor's dog buries a bone in your newly planted flower bed, can you see in it just the antics of your playful puppy? If your neighbor's son throws a rock through your window, does he become 'that brat headed for the reform school,' or can you see in him the reflection of your own son, just having fun and meaning no harm? This is your yardstick by which you must measure neighborly love. It should measure a full thirty-six inches from either side of the fence."

The Truth is—it is easy to criticize; it is much harder to understand. Resistance is increased as you try to prove which of your two egos is superior to the other. And your resistance prevents the meeting of minds that is so necessary for complete peace and understanding.

You will find that when you "bless" a condition, it cannot hurt you. Christ taught that it was wise to "Love thy neighbor as thyself," "Bless them that hurt you," "Do good unto those that despise you" and "Forgive those that trespass against you."

If He believes such attitudes are wise, then you should also, because then, like Daniel, you will "overcome your fear of the lions."

This may seem difficult for you at times, but with practice it becomes easy.

Two American women braved the jungles of Northern Peru to teach Christianity to the Indians. Tariri, chief of the head-hunting Shapra Indians said, "Now that I have learned about God and accepted Him, there will be no more killings by my tribe."

The approach they took was difficult but positive. They proved that love and *the Law of Non-Resistance* can overcome the most troublesome and cruel of men's habits when this *Law* is persistently followed.

The evil that men do and the oppressions some create will fade away when millions of people are encouraged to turn to *the Secret of Success,* send out more love and prayer and spiritual blessings.

Such evils and oppressions will then be overcome by the good that is sent out and those individuals who persist in such expressions of love "Shall be priests of God and of Christ, and shall reign with Him a thousand years."*

---

* Revelations 20:6

11

The Wonderful Gift of Choice

EVERY moment of your life, you are creating thoughts that will produce—either good luck or bad—happiness or misery—success or failure—love or hate.

The reason is—you have within your conscious mind the wonderful gift of choice.

With its help, you can direct your life in any way you choose. You can decide where you are going and what you will do when you get there. And it will help you to create conditions that will enable you to succeed or fail—according to the way you believe and in direct proportion to what you *desire*.

If the conditions you experience are unpleasant, you can improve them. If they are already good, you can make them better.

The choice is up to you.

You can choose confidence or despair, faith or fear, good will or distrust. You can move forward or stand still. You can choose to be a beggar or live in luxury. You can choose to be sick or well. You can choose to be happy or sad. You can choose to be wise or foolish.

You can choose to make money or lose it. You can choose to do better or quit. You can improve your life or stay in a rut.

You can continue with whatever you now have or you can

express more *faith* in God and the future and *believe* that new opportunities will open up for you so that you can make the progress you deserve.

But, if you choose despair and lack faith and lose hope, the negative thoughts you express can cause you to become old before your time. Their effect will be like holding your funeral before you are dead.

When you choose to be satisfied with lack of progress and grow old in spirit, then you violate the spiritual *Law of Evolution* and negative conditions will be created in your life that can lead to long periods of unhappiness. And you will also find that you must do without many of the things other people enjoy.

A large measure of the happiness you receive will result from giving. However, you do not have to give. You have a choice. You may prefer to withhold and keep whatever you own.

But whenever you choose to give anything you possess with a willing and open heart, notice how much better you feel. It is *the Law of Compensation* at work.

That fact is easy to prove. Give someone a smile and you will receive a smile in return. Give someone encouragement and you will, in return, be encouraged. Give someone help and you will receive help. Give someone love and you will receive love.

In spite of that fact, there will be times when you will be taken advantage of. Some people may laugh and say, "I got the better of him."

But that is not true. *They* made the wrong choice.

You must realize that everything in this world belongs to God. You are simply the steward appointed by Him over whatever you believe you own. When you pass away, someone else will, then, be the steward.

If you are a good steward and you choose to share your good fortune with others, the Infinite Spirit will reward you with many more material blessings in compensation for your willingness to give.

That is why you cannot lose by giving.

Many people, however, who do not know and understand the Source of Abundance will say, "If I could only have more money, I would be happy."

But no man or woman has ever secured a lasting type of happiness through the possession of large amounts of money. Nor can you find permanent happiness by attempting to control the lives of others or spending your time in the pursuit of sensual pleasures.

If money were a necessary ingredient for a happy life, then rich people would be the happiest of all. But many rich people I know are actually miserable. They often turn to liquor, gambling and wild parties in an effort to secure some form of pleasure that will satisfy them. Yet the more they chase such temporary pleasures, the more difficult it seems to be for them to secure true *peace of mind*.

Other people I know, who have very little money, enjoy peace of mind and find a great deal of satisfaction in simple things such as fishing, walking in the country or quietly sitting under a tree.

If you want to be happy—you must think happy thoughts. The reason is—true happiness originates within your own self. Yet millions of people try in vain to find peace of mind and satisfaction in material pleasures that can soon fade away.

The Truth is—the only moments of pleasure that last and can never be taken away from you are those you spend alone in communion with *the Secret of Success*.

That is what Christ meant when He said, "Lay up your treasures in Heaven, where neither moth nor rust doth corrupt, and where thieves do not break in and steal."*

_____
* Matthew 6:20

It is the highest form of security you can ever know.

An important man in Tarsus, named Saul, chose to "Lay up his treasures in Heaven" and became one of the most successful men the world has ever known.

Before he made this choice, his mind was so full of sinful thoughts that the average person today could not sin more often than he. Murder, lust, robbery and hate were all a part of his daily activities. As a man with a high position in the government, he was immune from prosecution and he could get away with more than the average citizen of Tarsus.

But Christ placed no permanent mark against the evil thoughts of Saul. Nor did He consider Saul's soul lost. Instead, He saw a man of great ability who, once he understood *the Truth,* could be trusted to carry out His work.

Christ did not say, "I will give Saul a few months or a few years to change and then—if he changes—I will make him one of my disciples." Christ looked beyond the sins Saul was committing and recognized the Divine Spirit of Good within.

He gave no thought to ways in which He would punish Saul. Instead, He knew that it does not take a long period of time for a man to change or to "be born again" and He believed that Saul could be taught that *Truth.*

He knew that Saul had the wonderful gift of choice.

He saw the Infinite Spirit of Creative Thought that Saul possessed and He asked him to choose the road that led to Glory and give up the one that led to degradation.

Today, we know that once sinful man as Paul—the greatest teacher of all the Apostles.

Through this wonderful gift of choice, Paul opened his mind to *the Truth* and he was able to change, improve himself and gain immortal fame.

When Paul made this choice, he found *the Secret of*

Success. He learned to understand this *Secret* and practiced it until it changed his life completely.

As Saul, the man with evil thoughts, he was destined to become infamous. As the Apostle, Paul, he became a respected leader of men and a Saint.

If he had chosen to remain Saul of Tarsus, he would have lived his life and been forgotten. No special recognition would have come to him. And, in spite of the wealth and influence he possessed in Tarsus, nothing of lasting value would have been given to the world.

As the Apostle Paul, he motivated millions of people to reach out and accept a better way of life. He inspired thousands of men and women to become Saints. He encouraged thousands of others to go into hostile lands and uncharted territory so that savages and heathens might know and understand the power and the glory of God.

And you, of course, can improve your life in much the same way because whatever you *desire* and believe in strongly enough will eventually come to pass.

If you believe in the best, the best will eventually come. That is why you should choose to believe in those things which can help you on towards success. But, if you believe in the worst or believe in failure, then you alone are to blame if troubles or failure should come to you. In fact, so long as you choose to keep your eyes toward the sun, the shadows will always fall behind you.

When you express worry and fear, you deny the presence of God within you. You prove to all those around you that you prefer, instead, to rely on the ideas and thoughts of mortal men.

But mortal men do not have the wisdom to "know and accomplish all things."

That is why worry and fear so often bring unhappy results.

When you maintain an attitude of *complete faith* in the wisdom and love of God, your mind is always poised and at ease. You feel there is no need to worry about temporary unpleasant conditions and you are able to work in greater harmony with God's plan.

Nowhere in the Bible do you find a single word that would cause you to believe in worry, fear, criticism, poverty or hate. Instead, you will find such expressions as "Of what are ye afraid, O ye of little faith," "Love thy neighbor as thyself" and "Stretch forth thy hand."

To the sinner, Christ did not say, "You must bear your punishment and spend many days in suffering."

No. He offered a choice. He said very clearly, "Arise, take up thy bed and walk" and "Thy sins shall be forgiven thee."

To repent of your sins means—*you must admit your mistakes immediately*—then, without hesitation, choose thoughts that are concerned with good things that can improve the world around you and offer more love and service to others. By changing your thoughts in this way, you prove that you want to change and improve your life.

Perhaps you find such an attitude difficult. And, for a while, it may be. But don't admit that you may fail. Don't allow yourself to say, "It can't be done." Those words are a poor choice. Instead, let your thoughts dwell on success.

Try it. Not once but continuously. Each day you practice the habit of thinking right thoughts and undertaking positive action, it becomes easier and easier.

There may be times when you feel sick, have an accident or face some financial problem. No matter how serious, its affects should be only temporary. If you will quietly relax and immediately turn the problem over to *the Secret of Success,* your Super-Conscious Mind will give your conscious mind an answer to that problem so you can overcome it and correct it.

The Truth is—when you have *complete faith* and *sincerely believe* in the ability and wisdom of your Super-Conscious Mind, you will experience many wonderful things in your life that other people may regard as "miracles."

New ideas will come to you that will open more doors of opportunity. And, if you choose to take full advantage of the opportunities you are given, you will never have to worry about where the money you need is coming from nor wonder how conditions in your life will improve.

You will also be able to concentrate on ways to reach your goal and never quit trying because you will *know* that ideas and solutions will come that will help you to find success.

Now that you understand why the right choice of thoughts are so important, you can see why negative thoughts of worry, fear, resentment, hate, anger and *partial belief* should be forgotten.

Your success will become easy if you will take the time to make many wise and proper decisions.

Here are a few questions you must continually ask yourself.

Am I certain I know why I am making this choice?

Do I understand and accept all of the responsibilities that are involved?

Am I sure that no one will be hurt, in any way, by my decision?

Am I certain I am working in complete harmony with God and the four spiritual Laws of Evolution, Compensation, Prosperity and Non-Resistance—or

Is it possible that the desire I have or the action I choose may be contrary to one of those important Laws?

With the above in mind, you will find that when you need to make a choice, it will be wise to turn immediately to *the Secret of Success* because God will never let you down— if you will ask Him in time for help.

If the conditions in your life are unpleasant, He will give you ideas to carry out that can help you make them better. If one door closes, another door will soon open. If you lose a job or a business deal, you will receive another—and the second may be better than the first.

Everything you need, everything you hope for will come to you if you will continue to believe in *the Secret of Success* and have *faith* that God's abundant wealth and wisdom will always help you find a way to supply your needs.

If God has the ability to create a baby, grow an apple tree and put the perfume within a rose, He is wise enough to help you solve any problem you may have.

"It sounds easy," you may say, "but you don't know all of the worries and problems I have."

The Truth is—worries and problems keep your mind upset because—

1. You think about them too much

2. You try too hard and

3. You allow those worries and problems to remain in your mind after they come in.

You must choose a better way.   You must replace those worries with *complete faith.*

You must seek help from the most dependable and wisest source possible—your Super-Conscious Mind.

While life is not perfect, it is really more pleasant than many people realize.   When things occur that irritate you, you can choose to let them make you unhappy or you can ignore them as temporary detours and say, "these too shall pass away."

In order to be successful, you must choose the thoughts and actions that will lead you on to success rather than failure. You must believe in yourself and your potential. And you must live in a positive way with positive thoughts and focus your mind on what you want to accomplish—even though some of the people around you may not believe it is possible.

One of the wisest choices you can make is to ask God for the ideas and encouragement you need. Let Him know you appreciate all of the wonderful events that occur each day. And let Him know you are eager and willing to be a part of the many interesting things that will happen tomorrow.

Then watch your "luck" increase.

Your choice of positive thoughts is important because, if you want to create conditions of permanent happiness and wealth, you must learn to spend more time in positive places with positive people who believe in God and have positive thoughts, a desire to serve others and believe in putting their positive thoughts into action.

The reason is—the consistent expression of God-inspired positive thoughts is the only way you can create dependable, long-lasting progress.

That is why you must spend little time with people who like to express negative thoughts. They cannot help you because their spirits are weak and they find it difficult to have enough of the good things necessary to enjoy life.

They say "No" too often or "It can't be done" and, if you associate with them for too long a period, such negative thoughts may cause you to agree with them.

But you lose too much when you agree with someone who says, "There's no use trying," "Everyone's against me," "Times are tough," "I don't feel well" or "How can anyone get along in a situation like this?"

Why get down in the dumps of despair with them?

All you can do with such people whose thoughts are negative is to try to cheer them up. Help them to choose happy, positive thoughts. Bless them and pray that, some day, they will desire to create a better way of life for themselves.

Do as Abraham Lincoln did for the unfortunate pig. Help them out of the mud of careless, negative thoughts onto more solid ground where successful, positive thoughts will prevail.

If you had a chain around your neck, you would remove it. And, in order to make progress, you must choose to throw off the chains of harmful thoughts that can hinder your progress. When the chains are removed, you will be able to move in the right direction and the success you seek will come more easily.

I remember an old friend named Harry. A man 57 years old who had always impressed me as being miserably unhappy and it showed plainly on his face. He looked grouchy and he acted grouchy.

He had a good job, but he was always passed by when promotions were given. He didn't seem to like anything. When he spoke, he used such negative words as, "It's no good," "I can't do it," "I don't believe," "I'm worried about," "If I could only," etc.

The more negative he became, the more unhappy he felt and looked.

But a miracle happened. I met Harry a few months ago and, instead of a gruff "hello," he gave me a big smile and a hearty handshake. He invited me for a cup of coffee and, with a tremendous amount of pride, he told me this story.

"You know how unhappy and grouchy I used to be. I thought everybody was wrong, except me. The more I thought it, the more I believed it. It would seem like sometime during my 57 years, I would have had a little happiness but, frankly, I had not.

"One day, a fellow at the office handed me a little book titled 'The Seven Day Mental Diet' by Emmet Fox and suggested I read it. At first, I was my same old hateful self and resented his suggestion. But, later in the day, a spark of curiosity struck me and I started to read. This little book showed me what a waste of time it was to have negative thoughts.

"It showed me how negative thoughts always produce unpleasant conditions. Then it explained how I could overcome those thoughts and change them into something more positive and better.

"They say, 'You can't teach an old dog new tricks,' but don't you believe it. I admit it wasn't easy. I had lived so long in such a terrible mental rut that I kept 'backsliding' into negative thoughts every hour or so. After a few days, I began to break the negative habit. I began to understand why the constant repetition of positive thoughts can help to make life more pleasant.

"I sure owe a lot to that 'Seven Day Mental Diet.' The fact is, I really feel 20 years younger. My food tastes better and I am beginning to get along with people.

"R. C.," he concluded, "it's wonderful."

When I took a more careful look at his formerly unhappy face, I found it had a smile you could appreciate. Yes, he did look several years younger.

Harry learned that positive thoughts are powerful thoughts. They get results that can be both beneficial and pleasant.

Negative thoughts, on the other hand, are weak and unable to create anything of value. In fact, a constant repetition of negative thoughts will tend to destroy things.

Why listen to them? Why repeat them?

Choose more positive thoughts like "Yes, I will," "I believe," "It can be done" and "Let's do it together." Such words can help you build a better life and make your day much brighter.

There is one basic cause for the tragedies and unpleasant conditions of the world. It is a lack of understanding of *the Secret of Success* and a failure to recognize that *the Law of Evolution* requires everyone to choose those ways that can lead onward and upward towards perfection in all things.

When you believe in the worst, you feel depressed. But, when you believe in the best, it gives you a feeling of new life and enthusiasm.

You will be rewarded with an awareness of more good all around you. And believing in the best will increase your power and ability to move ahead. It will also add to your happiness and make your success more certain.

"But," you may say, "how can I think happy thoughts when I have so many things to worry about?" or "So and so irritates me." Or you may add, "I have so many problems to think about, I haven't the time to be happy."

The answer, however, is easy. You do have a choice. It is all a matter of viewpoint and understanding.

The things you experience each day are not always what they seem. If you want to be happy, you must "Be of good cheer" and realize that "The Kingdom of Heaven is within."

This means in simple words—no one can make you happy and no one can make you unhappy unless you allow them to do so.

You have the wonderful gift of choice. You are "The master of your fate and the captain of your soul."

12

The Magical Power of Prayer

A RISTOTLE and Plato declared that the man who finds
his happiness in quiet thoughts and contemplation
(which we now call meditation and prayer) is the one who
is least dependent upon external circumstances.

Prayer is the conscious contact you make with your
Super-Conscious Mind. It never fails to uplift and
strengthen you because it is the most powerful single force
in the world.

And, tied together with *love* and *faith* and *belief*, prayer
can accomplish miracles when all else fails.

That is why it is the greatest confidence builder known to
man.

While that is true, many people with desperate needs,
never pray to God for help.

They say, "How can God possibly help me. I'll have to
ask someone I know." They have never learned how to
make a lasting contact with this Infinite Mind.

But enormous benefits can come to you when you learn
how to pray effectively.

When the chips are down and neither you nor your
friends can find an answer or a solution, when you have
moments of boredom and find you want to experience a
large measure of peace and contentment, the most logical
and practical thing you can do is turn to *the Secret of Suc-*

cess (the Infinite Source of all wisdom and power) not to some less efficient source as mortal man.

The Apostle Paul said, "Pray without ceasing." This means that, if you want to make certain you will benefit from *the Secret of Success,* you must be in close and constant contact with God—the source of all good—while you are eating, while you are out walking or driving, while you are grooming yourself for a date, while you are washing dishes or cleaning the house, while you are in a room full of people discussing a project, while you are preparing for an examination, while you are looking for a job and while you are getting ready to go to sleep.

Through the medium of prayer, you are asking God to be your partner and, when you have a partner who knows all the answers to every problem, it is logical that, with His Super-Conscious Mind helping your conscious mind, the two working together can do more than either one working alone.

You cannot afford to be too busy to pray any more than you can be too busy to be careful in whatever work you do.

Prayer does not *take* time, it saves time. And the time you spend in meditation and prayer is never wasted.

It makes your life richer, happier and more satisfying. And it makes it possible for you to be right when you might, without the benefits of prayer, be wrong.

Prayer does not cause you to lose anything. Instead, it helps you to gain many things of value.

Christ continuously performed miracles but he was successful because He spent long hours in prayer. And He proved the magical power of prayer because God always gave Him the guidance and help He needed.

It is reasonable to believe, therefore, that if Christ found it so necessary to pray in order to accomplish His miracles, then others with less experience and ability should find it wise and practical to do the same.

You may be certain that God always knows what you need. And, because He loves you, He is anxious to fill your needs. That is why He will never refuse your prayer if it is simple and sincere.

But your prayer must be based on a desire for whatever is fundamentally right. It must be unselfish and each prayer must end with the words, "Thy will, Father, not my will be done" and "Thank you, Father, I know you will help me."

The time you spend in prayer may be only a minute or two. But, during that time, you will be much closer to God. And, if you will humbly pray several times each day, the continuous habit will help you and the results you receive will be more pleasing and effective.

Such moments of prayer will give you added peace of mind and they will increase your ability to "accomplish all things."

There may be times, however, when it is difficult to overcome a problem by prayer. And that is especially true when you live in an area such as a large city, work in a factory or in a business where noise, confusion and distractions surround you.

Nevertheless, you can pray and receive an answer no matter where you are and no matter how much confusion may exist.

Soldiers have been known to pray sincerely and intensely in the midst of a hail of bullets and falling bombs. Several hundred passengers unable to get into the lifeboats on the ocean-liner Titanic prayed together amid the noise and confusion as the ship went down in the icy waters of the Atlantic. A mother pinned in a car wreck prayed for her unconscious husband and three babies as people milled around their car and ambulance sirens blared. And Otto

Graham, who played before 80,000 cheering fans as the star quarterback of the world champion Cleveland Browns football team, said "We got in a huddle before each game and prayed that God would protect us and help us to play our best."

You can pray and receive an answer on a moving train, on a jet plane or while driving your car. In fact, the more time you spend in such prayer, the more pleasant your trip will be and the more success you will have after you arrive at your destination.

When you pray and make beneficial contact with God, you will find there is no end to the ways in which His Infinite Intelligence can help you.

It is written, "I have weapons ye know not of; I have ways ye know not of; I have channels ye know not of."

Many people, however, do not trust the wisdom and unlimited ability of God — The Secret of All Success. They believe only what they can see after it has happened. Yet, the continually wonder why so little good comes to them. Others, cannot understand why so much of the good fortune and happiness they experience will often go away and leave them with so little.

The Creative Spirit of God that made you and all the world around you, has the ability and the intelligence to help you solve your problems and make your days more . But you must believe that fact and accept it as true.

No matter how critical a situation may seem or how difficult a problem may be, the Truth is—"The things which are impossible with men, are possible with God" and "God works in mysterious ways His wonders to perform."

That is why you should never try to tell God what to do nor how to solve your problem. The right answer will come as surely as the rising sun. But you must recognize it, accept it and carry out the directions you are given.

There may be times, however, when the answer you

receive will be the opposite of what you pray for.   It may even be "no" or "wait a few days."

The reason is—God may deny some of your small prayers because He wants to give you something better or more important in the future.

While you may find that difficult to understand, you must have *faith* and trust in His infinite wisdom.

God knows and God cares.   If His Infinite Mind has been wise enough to create you, It is also wise enough to sustain you.

His plan is to provide you with the best of everything. But He will give you only what you *believe* you will receive. And the more you *believe,* the more you will receive.

Even though your conscious mind may not agree that the way you are shown is the best way, you may rest assured that the answer you receive from your Super-Conscious Mind is the right one and your problem will be solved or the situation improved *at the right time.*

The answer you receive may not be the way you personally want it, but when you say, "Thy will be done," then you may be certain that, as time goes by, God's way will always prove to be the best.

Some people say, "If God is so powerful and so wise and so good, why does He allow us to go through all this suffering and cause us to work so hard?   Why doesn't He just provide all the comforts we need and make everyone happy?"

There are two reasons.   The first is—if there is no effort required, no suffering and no work to do, we would all become soft and lazy and careless.   Our muscles would be like jelly, our brains would be like mush and our boredom would be so great we would probably resort to long periods of sleep to keep from seeing too much of the things in which we would no longer have any interest.

The second reason is—we would find ourselves saying,

"If God really loves us, why doesn't He eliminate this boredom and give us something to do?"

So again it is easy to prove that God is like a loving father. Imagine how pitiful a child would grow up to be if his father gave him everything he asked for, took care of him every minute, never let him fall, never let his hands or clothes be soiled and never let him make a decision for fear he might make a mistake.

He would be a well-cared for child, but an insipid nobody.

It is easier to prove that the father who simply guides his son, points out right from wrong and allows him to grow through trial and error is actually expressing a greater amount of love.

He insists the baby should walk instead of crawl. He allows the child to exercise and play games to develop his body even though, at times, he may get hurt. As a teenager, the boy is allowed to deliver papers, work in a store or join the boy scouts.

And the result is—the father develops a man.

Every trial we experience, every discomfort, every drouth, every earthquake and every disease is God's way of forcing us to think and do better.

The student of the piano learns because the teacher insists on practice and each week the lesson gets a little harder until the pupil becomes a master.

So it is with life. We grow because we struggle, we learn and overcome.

Drouths occur so dams are built and irrigation is started, thereby improving the land. Disease occurs so men work many years to find a serum or drug that can eliminate that disease. More food is needed so men find ways to improve the soil and discover new areas for development.

God gives power to the weak and encouragement to the

faint. He is understanding love. And you may be sure that God knows what you need and He does not require explanations nor directions.

So, if you will relax and *believe* in His unfailing wisdom, He will provide you with the right answers and the right move to make.

But to receive the greatest amount of good, you must be tuned in and remain in contact with the Infinite Source of Good. You must wait for an idea or a lead to guide you. Then, when it comes, you must accept that gift from your Super-Conscious Mind and use every opportunity to carry out the idea or lead you are given.

If you fail to keep in contact with this Infinite Mind, the amount you receive will be less because you turn away too soon.

As you know, there is plenty of water behind the faucet in your kitchen. All you need to do is turn it on. While looking at the faucet, you see no water, but the water is there nevertheless.

That is how The Secret of Success appears to most people. They do not "see" the Infinite Source of All Supply so they find it is hard to believe this Source has an ever - abundant supply of everything — money, food, peace of mind, love and happiness always available to those who believe — if they will actively seek it and ask.

The Truth is—there are many benefits you will receive from prayer. But to produce favorable results, you must be spiritually alert. You must *believe* in the good things that God can create and have *a desire* for those things.

This means you must focus your attention on those God-inspired thoughts that will lead to prosperity, happiness and success. You must pray more and worry less.

Once you turn on the faucet that leads from your Super-Conscious Mind to your conscious mind and allow It to remain *open,* It will pour out a continuous supply of good. And you will quickly see how rich and dependable that supply can be.

When the faucet is closed, however, all you can receive is a trickle. As soon as you *close* your mind to this Infinite Source of Supply, then the amount you receive is reduced.

By turning your mind away from God, you make it difficult to achieve the amount of success you would like to have. For, "The Lord is good, a stronghold in the day of trouble; and He knoweth them that trust in Him."*

Everyone, at times, has sorrows and setbacks. Yet it is comforting to know that tragedy and suffering can, oftentimes, be a blessing. They cause you to think. And they can bring you an increase in resourcefulness.

Since that is true, many people believe that prayer is the most powerful and effective form of psychiatry. In fact, one of the most satisfying benefits of long periods of prayer is the serenity and calm that comes regardless of the turmoil and confusion that may exist around you.

No matter how tragic a situation may be, in spite of a serious accident, the death of loved ones, the inconvenience and horrors of war and even criticism, resentment and ill-will on the part of others, when you turn to prayer it has a magical way of making your life more pleasant and the tragedy easier to bear.

That is why a great many people know the beauty of inward peace. And they have secured that peace after they had undergone a great deal of suffering.

No matter how much they lost, no matter how much pain they had to bear, they were able to endure their hardship because they *believed* in the magical power of prayer and they turned to God for help.

Rather than cry or bemoan their fate, they turned imme-

* Nahem 1:7

diately to the Infinite Source of Good. And they were rewarded with the two most precious possessions they could ever own—*inward strength and peace of mind.*

They learned that, in the final analysis, no matter what might happen, the strength they need comes from "within." They can "take it" because, like Job in the Bible, they never lose faith.

The Truth is—prayer works. Many people, however, do not believe this. Friends may fail you, money may be hard to find and there may seem to be no way out of a problem. But the Bible suggests that we "Glory in tribulations; knowing that tribulations worketh patience; and patience, experience and experience, hope."*

Prayer, therefore, is a wonderful way to solve many problems. It will help to keep you forever on the path that leads to success.

And, by practicing the good habits of prayer, patience and faith, *the Secret of Success* will always help you find a way.

Furthermore, every effort you make to improve on whatever you see and do, causes God, as your Father, to love you more.

Another benefit of prayer is the way it helps to make you humble. While that may seem illogical, you must realize that Christ said, "The meek (those who are open-minded and believe in God) shall inherit the earth."

Why? The answer is—God loves those who love Him.

Paul was convinced of this for he wrote, "All things work together for good to them that love God."

If you will spend a few minutes each day and, like Solomon, pray for wisdom and understanding, you will prevent many years of possible mistakes.

Many people, who pray, however, do not choose that

---

* Romans 5:3

attitude. Oftentimes, they never stop to listen. They are so busy trying to express themselves or make their wishes known they fail to take the time to wait and receive an answer.

The poor sinner in Luke 18:11 pleading for mercy seems weak and insecure. But *the Truth is*—his great respect and love for God gained greater attention from His Father than that of the proud Pharisee who could see no fault with himself.

With his humble and reverent attitude, the sinner could learn and grow and perfect himself.

But the Pharisee, unfortunately, could learn very little. Through his proud and arrogant manner, his self-righteous mind said, "I'm satisfied" and he closed it to further good.

To a material-minded person who is interested in money, power, fame and pleasure, prayer is called *desire*.

To one who has a religious background and wants to secure the more permanent and dependable values in life, prayer is called *talking with God*.

But, in each case, whether you call it desire or talking with God, the result often seems to be the same.

The reason is—when one individual has *a strong desire* and the other believes in talking with God, they are both obeying *the Law of Evolution*—which is to look up, move forward and grow.

That is why a person who does not go to church or observe any of the doctrines and beliefs of a church can still have a form of material success.

He can earn large amounts of money, own a fine home, have a large business and possess many of the things he *desires*.

But such outward forms of success are only temporary because they are based on money—which can fade for many reasons. They cannot last as long nor bring as much peace of mind and contentment as those things which are spiritual and comes from knowing that God is the Source of All Good. That is why He is — The Secret of Success.

Fortunately, God allows many enlightened men and women to have large incomes and possess both material wealth and spiritual wealth. As compensation for their good fortune, they should practice the art of tithing and give generously to help promote *the Truth* and help others to understand *the Secret of Success.*

Prayer is made easier when you know how to communicate with God. It gives you a tremendous uplift and satisfaction that is possible from no other source. But, like Job, you must persevere. And the more often you communicate, the easier it is to remain calm and peaceful in the midst of confusion.

You must keep your faith alive and constant—no matter what happens.

When Job was visited by his friends they said, "Why do you put up with all this torment."

Job replied, "Even though He slay me, yet will I trust Him."*

The calmness that comes when you readily turn to meditation and prayer is a beneficial effect that is more soothing and certainly more economical than tranquilizers, cigarettes or dope.

The reason is—"Thou will keep him in perfect peace whose mind is stayed on Thee."†

And the more often you turn to prayer for such calmness and peace of mind, the greater the habit becomes and the more effective will be the result.

In fact, such a habit will do so much to strengthen your spirit and cleanse your soul of any doubts and fears, you will never find the need to turn to therapeutic agents, psychoanalysts or drugs.

---

* Job 13:15
† Isaiah 26:3

And, if you will "Pray without ceasing," your relief from anxiety and torment will be permanent.

"But," some people say, "What cannot be cured must be endured." That is not true. Such a thought is negative and negative thoughts will always handicap your efforts. They hinder your progress because they are contrary to what God wants you to experience through His spiritual *Law of Evolution.*

It is impossible to think clearly while your conscious mind is filled with fears and doubts and worries.

They are not necessary and they are based on your will rather than God's will.

God's plan is always positive—never negative. That is why you can say of such negative, unpleasant conditions, "With your help, Father, I know they too shall pass away."

When you pray with the knowledge and understanding that "According to thy faith, be it unto you," you must always be ready for surprises.

If your faith is weak or insincere, there will be times when everything seems to go wrong. And you may feel that you are held back instead of helped.

But such a feeling should cause you to communicate more often with God and increase the amount of your faith.

Such an attitude will prove to be wise because "Whosoever putteth his trust in the Lord shall be safe."*

In the year 1848, the Mormons had raised a good crop around their new homes near Salt Lake City. Just before harvest, a plague of locusts descended and ruthlessly began to devour the crop their sweat and toil had produced.

If this harvest was destroyed, then many of those in the community would starve because winter was coming. They had already endured great hardship while driving their

---

* Proverbs 29:25.

wagons across the great plains and over the rugged mountains. There was little left in their storehouse. Transportation was slow and it was several hundred miles to the nearest supply center to bring in additional food.

But the Mormons had *faith*. They knew that God would send them help—if every one of them prayed together.

They *believed* in the truth of God's words, "I have weapons ye know not of," "Ask and ye shall receive" and "As ye believe so shall it be done unto you."

Those fine people had tremendous faith and it was soon proved.

God heard their prayers and an army of sea gulls came, swallowed up the locusts and gorged themselves.

Salt Lake City is 460 air miles from the sea. Surely this was a miracle as great as many of those performed by Christ.

The Mormons were grateful for God's response and they promised Him they would never forget it. A statue, therefore, was erected to the sea gull so that it would always remind them of the magical power of prayer and positive belief backed by faith.

The Mormons could easily have said, "It's too late. Nothing can save our crop now." But they knew that everything works out for the best—provided you have faith, never give up hope and say, "Thy will, Father, not my will, be done."

Another beneficial result of prayer is the way it helps to heal those who are mentally sick and increases the vitality of those who are physically unwell.

As it brings about improvement, it fulfills the promise Christ made when He said, "I am come that ye may have life, and have it more abundantly."

One night a few years ago, my car ran out of gas. While pouring in enough to get started, an automobile ran off the road and smashed me against the back of my car. My leg was nearly torn off. My elbow was shattered and my arm was broken in several places.

During the many months I was recuperating, I had no income, my assets were dwindling and I had to give up a job with an income of $2,000 per month.

The man who hit me had no personal liability insurance and everything looked bad. But I had faith. Six months after I was out of the hospital, I found another job that was better, in many ways, than the one I had regretted losing. My income was greater and I found myself wiser because of the increased faith I possessed.

My elbow is still deformed from the accident, but now I realize that a strong arm is not as important in life as a strong *desire* and a strong *belief*.

If you want your prayers to be successful, you must be honest and sincere. You must express no hate nor malice towards anyone. It is "the pure in heart," Christ said, "who shall see God." That means that the Infinite Spirit of Good is more willing to help you when the desire you have comes from an honest expression filled with love.

As your Father, God understands and knows why you make mistakes. He overlooks many things. But He wants you to realize that all of the people around you are His children also.

That is why, in His eyes, everyone you know and meet should be treated with courtesy and respect.

If you came from a large family and you were to hit one of your brothers or sisters, or hate one of them, or wish one of them bad luck in any way, your earthly father would not willingly give you something just because you asked for it.

He would say, "Apologize to your brother or sister first, wish him luck, help him—do not hurt him—then I will grant your wish."

And your earthly father would watch you carefully to see,

first, if you did as he asked and second, whether your attitude was sincere and you truly were sorry for your thoughts and actions and would not attack or dislike your brother or sister again.

That is why God looks on you as one of His children. If you are good, kind and considerate, He will help you sooner and with greater love than if He has to find some way to get you to realize your shortcomings, admit your mistakes and secure your promise to Him that you will do better.

As soon as you come to Him in a humble, loving attitude, conditions improve. Your desires arc granted and your life moves along more smoothly.

So you can see that it really pays to be good whether you are one year old or one hundred.

Christ knew how to pray and He always found it easy to receive an answer.

His disciples, therefore, said, "When you pray, something happens, but when we pray nothing happens. Teach us, therefore, how to pray."

Then Christ gave them the secret of how to pray successfully. There were five points he continually stressed:

1. "When thou prayest, enter into thy closet, and when thou has shut thy door, pray to thy Father which is in secret; and thy Father which seeth in secret shall reward thee openly."*

In brief, Christ meant—make certain that you get away from all worldly confusion. Find a place where you can be quiet.

If you are in a busy, noisy place, you must shut your mind to the noise, then relax and turn your mind inward toward "the Father within" as you learned in Chapter 5.

* Matthew 6:6

2. "Use not vain repetitions as the heathen do."* This means you should not idly repeat the words of someone else or read a prayer out of a book.

Reading or following someone else's words can give you guidance, but your prayer is more sincere and effective when the words you speak are your own and they come from your heart.

3. "Your Father knoweth what things ye have need of, before ye ask Him."† This means that you do not need to explain the details of your problem to God, nor do you have to wonder if He understands, nor should you *hope* He hears you.

You may be certain—He does.

4. "Forgive us our debts as we forgive our debtors . . . for if ye forgive men their trespasses, your Heavenly Father will also forgive you, but if ye forgive not their trespasses, neither will your Father forgive your tresspasses."‡

5. This is the most important one of all. You must acknowledge God's wisdom and realize that, while your desire or prayer may be strong, it may not be right.

God knows best and, like Christ in the garden of Gethsemene, you must always say, "Nevertheless, Father, not my will, but Thy will be done."

Then, when your prayer is answered, give thanks to *the Secret of Success* and be grateful.

---

* Matthew 6:7
† Matthew 6:8
‡ Matthew 6:12–15